Media Controversies

Media Controversies

Edited by
Lester A. Sobel

Facts On File, Inc.
460 Park Avenue South, New York, N.Y. 10016

Media
Controversies

© Copyright, 1981, by Facts On File, Inc.

All rights reserved. No part of this book may be reproduced in any form without the permission of the publisher except for reasonably brief extracts used in reviews or scholarly works.
Published by Facts On File, Inc.,
460 Park Avenue South, New York, N.Y. 10016

Library of Congress Cataloging in Publication Data

Sobel, Lester A
  Media controversies.

    Includes index.
  1.   Government and the press—United States—History—20th century.   I. Title.
PN4738.S7   071′.3   80-22880

9 8 7 6 5 4 3 2 1
PRINTED IN
THE UNITED STATES OF AMERICA

Media Controversies

Introduction

Freedom & Controversy

NEWS, INFORMATION, OPINION, commentary, analysis and advertising. By and large, these are the principal elements of the non-entertainment substance of newspapers, television and radio programs and magazines. This material can be about such potentially controversial issues as politics, government activities, taxes, business, labor, international relations, war, personalities, crime, education, science, the arts, and the news media as well. Controversy often flares even over such media content as sports and entertainment.

Where there is dispute about a topic, there is certain to be strong interest in the manner in which publications and broadcasts present it. Coverage of an election campaign in the media could well determine who will be elected President or what the political complexion of Congress will be. Advertising and public relations campaigns in the media can conceivably make the difference between enormous profit or bankruptcy for many competitive corporations. It would not be much of an exaggeration to say that there are situations—such as in the presentation of a play or motion picture—in which media reviewers can decide which production shall live and which shall die. Under these circumstances, broadcasting licenses and popular periodicals can confer power and wealth on the owners of television and radio stations and newspapers and magazines. The licensing and ownership of the media, therefore, also become centers of competition and controversy.

Where the news media is concerned, however, a further complexity and cause of controversy exists. This complication arises from the long struggle for "freedom of the press." When criticism or conflict involves the media, some participant is almost certain to charge, often with good cause, that his right of "freedom of the press" is under attack.

The following partial list indicates issues over which media controversies have been fought, and in probably no instance will a reader have much trouble in determining how a "freedom of the press" issue is involved:

- Conflicts of media rights with other rights. Examples include an accused person's right to a fair trial as opposed to the media's asserted right to print or broadcast material that may prejudice potential jurors.
- The demand for a "newsman's privilege," or "shield," that would permit reporters to refuse to reveal their sources of information to grand juries or other judicial or police inquisitors.
- The media's dissemination of military, diplomatic or intelligence secrets whose disclosure, according to government complaints, would jeopardize security, hamper foreign relations or endanger the lives of intelligence personnel.
- Censorship and alleged government attempts to control, coerce, intimidate or manipulate the media.
- Political use of the media.
- The use of news personnel by the intelligence agencies.
- The growth of the media and media power and their increasing concentration in the hands of fewer and fewer owners.
- The apparent lack of effective restraint on the misuse of media power.
- The emergence of television as the dominant news medium.
- Self-regulation of the media.
- Unfair or inaccurate presentation of material by the media, including charges of staging news events.
- The declining effect of libel law.
- The emergence of the "new journalism," characterized by newsmen's "advocacy" as opposed to objectivity.
- The purported preponderance of sex and violence on television.
- Deceptive advertising of products ranging from automobiles and

Introduction

gasoline to breakfast foods and pharmaceuticals.
• Methods used by the media in the competition for viewers and readers.

The news media—or "the press"—is generally seen as having two major components, print media and electronic media. In testimony before the Senate Subcommittee on Constitutional Rights February 8, 1972, Andrew Heiskell, chairman of the board of the Time, Inc. magazine-publishing organization, protested an increase in postal rates for magazines as having serious implications for a free press. "Of course," he said, "the American press today consists of four major elements—newspapers, magazines, radio and television. An effective national press must be a composite of these media, for each performs a distinct service and no one of them could substitute for any other. Magazines and network broadcasting, particularly television, speak to a national audience, while both newspapers and radio tend to be more local in their coverage."

The media, however, need not be considered limited to printed and electronic dissemination. Motion pictures—now a staple of the television industry—have long been said to deserve protection of the type accorded the press. Justice William O. Douglas of the Supreme Court held in 1948 (in *United States* v. *Paramount Pictures*): "We have no doubt that moving pictures, like newspapers and radio, are included in the press whose freedom is guaranteed by the First Amendment."

Henry Grunwald asserts in the July 16, 1979 issue of *Time* magazine that one reason "journalists are so worried, even perhaps slightly paranoid, about the loss of their freedoms is that these rights have never been very secure. . . ." He recalls that in sixteenth century England, members of the press "were constantly in danger of imprisonment or torture, even of beheading, hanging and burning at the stake, sometimes for refusal to reveal the source of confidential information." Although conditions for journalists were improved in America, Grunwald concedes, their calling remained "a high-risk trade" in the New World as well. "Editors were always in danger of being challenged to duels or horsewhipped or beaten up by gangs," he continued. "Tarring and feathering editors was a popular pastime" on the frontier, and "symbolically, . . . it still is."

The history of journalism in America—and the issue of freedom of the press on this continent—go back as far as 1690, when the New World's first newsletter, *Publick Occurrences Both Foreign and Domestic,* made its appearance in Boston. The first issue was the last. The royal governor of Massachusetts suppressed it immediately as having been issued by its publisher, Benjamin Harris, "without the least... countenance of authority." The newsletter also recorded items of doubtful accuracy that the governor considered unfitting for publication: reports on the corruption of Indians by colonists and on the French king's alleged seduction of his daughter-in-law.

The publication of newspapers without countenance of authority or fear of suppression had to wait until the American Revolution. Before the Revolution, however, there were repeated cases of publishers jailed for "wicked lyes and slanders upon Government," for "sundry vile insinuations against His Majesty's rightful and lawful authority" and for "inflaming the minds of His Majesty's subjects." Yet publishers continued to face these risks and to produce periodicals that provoked authority by publicizing unpalatable truths.

The case that is best remembered is that of John Peter Zenger, publisher of the *New York Weekly Journal.* Zenger was imprisoned in 1734 on a charge of "seditious libel" for publishing criticism of William Cosby, the colonial governor. After nine months in prison, Zenger was brought to trial in August 1735. The judge, appointed by Cosby, Zenger's accuser, instructed the jury that "it is necessary for all governments that the people should have a good opinion of it. And nothing can be worse to any government than to endeavor to procure animosities; as to the management of it, this has always been looked upon as a crime, and no government can be safe without it be punished." Zenger's defense was that his criticisms of the governor—which included allegations of appointing corrupt officials—were true and that printing the truth about the government was not criminal. This defense was argued for him by Andrew Hamilton, who called on the jury to secure "that to which nature and the laws of our country have given us a right—the liberty of both exposing and opposing arbitrary power (in these parts of the world at least) by speaking and writing truth." The jury agreed and freed Zenger.

The theory of freedom of the press under British commom law before the American Revolution is most authoritatively described in Sir William Blackstone's *Commentaries on the Law of England:* "The liberty of the press is, indeed, essential to the nature of

Introduction

a free state; but this consists in laying no *previous* restraints upon publication, and not in freedom from censure for criminal matter when published. Every free-man has an undoubted right to lay what sentiments he pleases before the public; to forbid this, is to destroy the freedom of the press; but if he publishes what is improper, mischievous, or illegal, he must take the consequences of his own temerity. To subject the press to the restrictive power of a licenser, as was formerly done, both before and since the revolution, is to subject all freedom of sentiment to the prejudices of one man, and make him the arbitrary and infallible judge in all controverted points in learning, religion and government. But to punish (as the law does at present) any dangerous or offensive writings, which, when published, shall on a fair and impartial trial be adjudged of a pernicious tendency, is necessary for the preservation of peace and good order, of government and religion, the only solid foundation of civil liberty. Thus the will of the individuals is still left free; the abuse only of the free will is the object of legal punishment. Neither is any restraint laid upon freedom of thought or inquiry; liberty of private sentiment is still left; the disseminating, or making public, of bad sentiments, destructive to the ends of society, is the crime which society corrects."

In the United States, the media's basic guarantee is in the First Amendment to the Constitution: *Congress shall make no law* respecting an establishment of religion, or prohibiting the free exercise thereof; or *abridging the freedom* of speech, or *of the press;* or the right of the people peaceably to assembly, and to petition the Government for a redress of grievances [italics added by editor]." This guarantee is part of the "Bill of Rights"—the first ten amendments to the Constitution—which was ratified December 1, 1791. Thomas I. Emerson points out in *The System of Freedom of Expression* (1970) that "The precise meaning of the First Amendment at the time of its adoption is a matter of some dispute." He deduces that the amendment's "fundamental meaning" has come to be a guarantee of "an effective system of freedom of expression suitable for the present time." The Supreme Court, however, "has never developed any comprehensive theory of what that constitutional guarantee means," Emerson says. It has used various tests, which have produced chaotic and "unhappy results," Emerson finds.

One of the Americans most prominent in the campaign for a declaration on freedom of the press—and in fact for the addition of a "Bill of Rights" to the Constitution—was Thomas Jefferson. In an often quoted 1787 letter, Jefferson said: "The basis of our government being the opinion of the people, the first object should be to keep that right; and were it left to me to decide whether we should have a government without newspapers, or newspapers without a government, I should not hesitate a moment to prefer the latter. But I should mean that every man should receive those papers, and be capable of reading them. . . ."

In a letter to Washington in 1792, Jefferson wrote: "No government ought to be without censors; and where the press is free, no one ever will. If virtuous, it need not fear the fair operation of attack and defense. . . ."

As time passed, Jefferson became increasingly disenchanted with an abusive and often untruthful press, but he continued to champion a free press. The Virginia and Kentucky Resolutions of 1799, in which James Madison joined Jefferson as co-author, said: "Some degree of abuse is inseparable from the proper use of everything; and in no instance is this more true than in that of the press. It has accordingly been decided by the practice of the States, that it is better to leave a few of the noxious branches, to their luxuriant growth, than by pruning them away, to injure the vigor of those yielding the proper fruits. And can the wisdom of this policy be doubted by any who reflect, that to the press alone, checquered as it is with abuses, the world is indebted for all the triumphs which have been gained by reason and humanity, over error and oppression; who reflect, that to the same beneficent source, the United States owe much of the lights which conducted them to the rank of a free and independent nation; and which have improved their political system into a shape so auspicious to their happiness."

In 1807, after more than a term and a half as President, Jefferson seemed to have more to say about the evils of the press than about the need for press freedom. ". . . a suppression of the press," he wrote, "could not more completely deprive the nation of its benefits than is done by its abandoned prostitution to falsehood. Nothing can now be believed which is seen in a newspaper. Truth itself becomes suspicious by being put into that polluted vehicle. . . . I will add, that the man who never looks into a newspaper is better informed than he who reads them; inasmuch as he who knows nothing is nearer the truth than he whose mind is filled with falsehoods and errors. . . ."

The guarantee of press freedom in America came into question even before the First Amendment had survived its seventh year. In the troubled summer of 1798, with the Republic seemingly on the verge of collapse, the Federalist majority in Congress sought to stifle opposition by the enactment of the Alien and Sedition Acts. The Sedition Act, approved by the Senate ironically July 4, made it a crime to publish "any false, scandalous and malicious writing" against the government, Congress or President. Several opponents of the Administration were fined or imprisoned under this law for daring to put into print their criticisms of those in power. It was reported that many others waived their First Amendment right to publish their views for fear of prosecution. The Alien and Sedition Acts were ultimately repealed and never subjected to a court test of their constitutionality. Today's constitutional specialists, and some who preceded them, seem largely to agree that these measures were in violation of the First Amendment.

It appears clear to many commentators, however, that the First Amendment was not intended, no more than the British common law that fathered it, to give sanction to all publication.

Justice Felix Frankfurter of the Supreme Court held to this effect in a 1951 opinion (in the case of *Dennis* v. *United States*): "The historic antecedents of the First Amendment preclude the notion that its purpose was to give unqualified immunity to every expression that touched on matters within the range of political interest. The Massachusetts Constitution of 1780 guaranteed free speech; yet there are records of at least three convictions for political libels obtained between 1799 and 1803. The Pennsylvania Constitution of 1790 and the Delaware Constitution of 1792 expressly imposed liability for abuse of the right of free speech. [James] Madison's own state put on its books in 1792 a statute confining the abusive exercise of the right of utterance. And it deserves to be noted that in writing to John Adams' wife, [Thomas] Jefferson did not rest his condemnation of the Sedition Act of 1798 on his belief in unrestrained utterance as to political matter. The First Amendment, he argued, reflected a limitation upon federal power, leaving the right to enforce restrictions on speech to the states. . . . 'The law is perfectly well settled,' this court [the Supreme Court] said over fifty years ago, 'that the first ten amendments to the Constitution, commonly known as the Bill of Rights, were not intended to lay down any novel principles of government but simply to embody certain guarantees and immunities which we had inherited from our English ancestors, and which had from time immemorial, been subject to certain well-recognized exceptions, arising from the necessities of the case. In incorporating these principles into fundamental law, there was no intention of disregarding the exceptions, which continued to be recognized as if they had been formally expressed.' That this represents the authentic view of the Bill of Rights and the spirit in which it must be construed has been recognized again and again in cases that have come here [before the Supreme Court] within the last fifty years."

As late as 1907 (in the case of *Patterson* v. *Colorado*) the Supreme Court still left undecided the question of whether the Fourteenth Amendment extended the First Amendment's guarantees and prohibitions to the states. Justice Oliver Wendell Holmes cited at that time an earlier finding that the main purpose of "these constitutional provisions is 'to prevent all such *previous restraints* upon publications as had been practiced by other governments,' and they do not prevent the subsequent punishment of such as may be deemed contrary to the public welfare." Holmes noted that "the preliminary freedom extends as well to the false as to the true; the subsequent punishment may extend as well to the true as to the false. This was the law of criminal libel apart from statute in most cases, if not in all." Holmes said, however, perhaps hopefully, that "there is no constitutional right to have all general propositions of law once adopted remain unchanged."

It was not until 1925 that the Supreme Court (in *Gitlow* v. *New York*) asserted that the Fourteenth Amendment did extend the First Amendment's requirements to the states. "For present purposes," the ruling said, "we may and do assume that freedom of speech and of the press, which are protected by the First Amendment from abridgment by Congress—are among the fundamental principle rights and 'liberties' protected by the due process clause of the Fourteenth Amendment from impairment by the states." Six years later (in *Near* v. *Minnesota*), this *dictum* was specifically applied to freedom of the press.

Censorship of some speech or publication was not considered barred by the First Amendment, as Frankfurter recalled in his opinion in *Dennis* v. *United States*. Supreme Court Justice Frank Murphy had also noted, in 1942 (in *Chaplinsky* v. *New Hamp-*

Introduction

shire), that "there are certain well-defined and narrowly limited classes of speech, the prevention and punishment of which have never been thought to raise any constitutional problem. These include the lewd and obscene, the profane, the libelous, and the insulting or 'fighting' words—those which by their very utterance inflict injury or tend to incite an immediate breach of the peace." He added that "it has been well observed that such utterances are no essential part of any exposition of ideas. . . ."

The following year Justice Robert H. Jackson (in *West Virginia State Board of Education* v. *Barnette*) held it "a commonplace that censorship or suppression of expression of opinion is tolerated by our Constitution only when the expression presents a clear and present danger of action of a kind the state is empowered to prevent and punish."

The twentieth century added complications to freedom-of-the-press controversy with the introduction of the electronic media. Opening a series of press-freedom hearings by the Senate Subcommittee on Constitutional Rights in September 1971, Senator Sam Ervin of North Carolina noted that "the Founding Fathers did not contemplate the media of radio and television when they wrote the First Amendment." Nevertheless, Ervin held, "their reasons for protecting the printed press from government control apply equally to the broadcast media. More people get their news from radio and television today than from any other single source. . . . If First Amendment principles are held not to apply to the broadcast media, it may well be that the constitutional guarantee of a free press is on its death bed."

"Great confusion surrounds the federal statutes, regulations, and the few court decisions which affect broadcasting," Ervin continued. "Congress enacted the Radio Act of 1927 and the Communications Act of 1934 to prevent the air waves from being flooded with such a host of voice that the medium of broadcasting would be rendered useless. Whatever government regulation of broadcasting was authorized, it was only for the purpose of securing the most effective use of available air waves and communications technology. . . . [But] this limited authority with respect to broadcasting has . . . expanded . . . to the point that many broadcasters believe principles of freedom of the press no longer have significance with respect to broadcasting. . . ."

"Our Founding Fathers were wise enough to know that there is no way to give freedom of speech and press to the wise and deny it to fools and knaves," Ervin asserted. "Certainly, they did not intend for the government to decide who were the wise and who were the knaves." He observed that "it is easier to preach freedom of the press than it is to practice it." And he warned that "in the midst of controversies which seem to us now as earth-shaking, we tend to lose sight of the higher issues at stake."

Basic changes have taken place in the American press ince *Publick Occurrences* of 1690, since the Revolution and "over the past twenty years," as John B. Oakes, former editor of the editorial page of *The New York Times,* pointed out May 17, 1978 in the first Frank E. Gannett Memorial Lecture.

"Hardly one hundred years ago, we were in the golden age of personal journalism," Oakes said. "It took little capital to start a newspaper, little readership to keep it alive. What it did take was a strong, articulate editor who had a distinct point of view and was willing and able to express himself with force and cogency. This was the era of the partisan personalities of American journalism. . . ." This personal journalism has been largely replaced by "the journal of information." American newspapers "have increasingly moved toward a kind of standardization," Oakes reported, and "have also become big business, a development that has already had and will doubtless continue to have a subtly adverse effect on both public and judicial perception of the First Amendment's protection of press freedom." Control of the press has become increasingly concentrated, he continued. "Huge corporate conglomerates" have replaced much individual ownership, and competition among local newspapers has declined to a low point. The newspaper audience has been changing and decreasing for various reasons, among them the shift to reliance on television news and, Oakes asserted, "above all, the loss of credibility in all institutions, including the press."

Max Kampelman, Washington lawyer who has served as counsel and adviser for such diverse powers as the late Senator Hubert H. Humphrey and the United States delegation to the United Nations, describes the American press as "perhaps the second most powerful institution in the country next to the Presidency." Writing in 1978 in *Policy Review,* in an article entitled "The Power of the Press: A Problem for Our Democracy," Kampelman adds in a footnote that a 1974 survey had found a cross-section of national leaders ranking television "ahead of the White House as the

Introduction

country's number one power center." The press, he continues, "is characterized by few, if any, effective restraints."

Kampelman asserts that the framers of the Constitution did not mean freedom of the press to lead to "a press possessed of very nearly unrestrained license." The First Amendment, specifically forbidding Congress to abridge freedom of the press by law, was intended as a prohibition aimed at the national government and not a restriction of action by the states, Kampelman holds. He quotes Thomas Jefferson as having written to his wife: "While we deny that Congress have the right to control the freedom of the press, we have ever asserted the right of the states, and their exclusive right to do so."

Journalists, like other people, are hardly ever unanimous in any view, including opinions on the danger press freedom faces in America. Charles Shaw, a newspaper and radio journalist for forty-seven years, observed in the *New Hope* (Pa.) *Gazette* April 26, 1979 that "governments of the United States have been chipping away at freedom of the press since World War II." Thomas Griffith reported in the June 18, 1979 issue of *Times,* however, that some newspaper editors "have grown sensitive about how often the press cries wolf over the First Amendment. . . . Each court attempt to redefine the press's responsibility in libel suits or criminal trials isn't necessarily tearing the First Amendment to tatters. . . ." James J. Kilpatrick had asserted in his syndicated column Oct. 10, 1971 that "over the thirty-odd years of my own professional experience, First Amendment freedoms have expanded, not contracted." Newsmen were no longer "chilled" by threats of suit for libel. In his early newspaper days, Kilpatrick said, "an editor could write gingerly of 'planned parenthood' and 'social diseases'" whereas "even the girl reporters" now write "of contraceptives and syphilis, and nobody blinks."

According to Sidney Zion, a lawyer as well as a journalist, the Supreme Court under Chief Justice Warren E. Burger "reshaped the Bill of Rights," and Burger Court "interpretations of the First Amendment . . . led to the greatest constitutional confrontation of the 1970s—that between the news media and the courts. . . ." Writing in the Nov. 18, 1979 issue of *The New York Times Magazine,* Zion asserts that during the relatively tranquil 1970s, the press suffered "a judicial battering that has been more serious, and more fundamental, than the assaults that were mounted in more parlous times." Zion found "the reporter . . . being tossed into jail for refusing to disclose his or her confidential sources," the newsroom "held to be fair game for ransacking by police officers," a "reporter's inner thoughts . . . being opened for discovery by plaintiffs in libel suits." "Finally," wrote Zion, "the reporter's rights to cover trials was held to be nonexistent. . . ."

Three journalism historians were asked by the Gannett Foundation's advisory committee on education to discuss the question of whether a constitutional link exists between the right to publish news and the right to gather news. The December-January 1978 issue of *The Bulletin* of the American Society of Newspaper Editors reports a unanimous verdict that "while our right to publish stands secure, our 'right' to gather does not."

Professor Don R. Pember of the University of Washington held in his article in *The Bulletin* that "there is no official record which suggests that the First Amendment was intended to grant a right to gather the news." He found no evidence, "either historical or legal," he wrote, to support "the notion that there shouldn't be a right of access under freedom of the press."

Professor Harold L. Nelson of the University of Wisconsin wrote that he could not "name any one of the Founding Fathers who had any notion that the First Amendment might include the right to gather news freely." None of the standard law-of-the-press texts of the period 1920-50 "even mentions fact-gathering and the First Amendment," he said.

Professor Donald M. Gillmore of the University of Minnesota held that "those who believe that free press and free news-gathering are inseparable are not totally wrong; they simply overstate their case." He reported that there was "some good language in lower state and federal courts" for an implied right to gather news. But he concluded that such court language "does not establish that right's constitutional existence."

James Russell Wiggins, publisher of the *Ellsworth* (Me.) *American* and former executive editor of the *Washington Post,* rejected the findings of the journalism historians. In a statement written for the ASNE *Bulletin* (and printed also in the December 30, 1978 edition of *Editor & Publisher),* Wiggins held that "the right to get information has been asserted and defended under the general theory of popular government, under the specific provisions relating to open courts, and under the First Amendment." Wiggins quoted Harold Cross as writing in *The Right To Know* (1953) that

Introduction

the First Amendment embraces, "if indeed it does not require, the inclusion of a right of access to information of government without which the freedom to print could be fettered into futility." He denied that the framers of the Constitution "intended to provide for freedom to disseminate such information but to deny freedom to acquire it."

Not all criticisms of the press are entirely serious, however controversial they may be. David E. Lilienthal wrote of an incident in October 1945, when he was chairman of the Tennessee Valley Authority and soon to become the first head of the Atomic Energy Commission. Lilienthal asked President Harry S. Truman whether he felt it was permissible for him to accept invitations to make speeches. Truman's perhaps facetiously intended answer (as recorded in *The Journals of David E. Lilienthal,* Volume II, 1964) was: "It is perfectly all right to accept them [invitations]. . . . [T]hat's the only way the people will get to know the facts—they sure won't know them through the newspapers."

The late Mayor Richard J. Daley of Chicago, however, was undoubtedly serious when he complained about reporters: "They have vilified me, they have crucified me; yes, they have even criticized me."

THE PURPOSE OF THIS BOOK IS to chronicle the important developments in controversy about the news media during the past puzzling decade. A major source of information is the record compiled by FACTS ON FILE in its ongoing examination of world affairs. The controversial nature of much of this material is obvious, but, as in all FACTS ON FILE books, a conscientious effort was made to keep this volume free of bias and to produce a balanced and accurate reference work.

LESTER A. SOBEL

Freeport, N.Y.
August, 1981

The Media Versus the Nixon Administration

The Adversary Role of the Media

The press—electronic and print—performs several functions in the American system. It informs. It enlightens. It entertains. It complains. It persuades. It advises. It teaches. It interprets. It advocates. It attacks. The services of the media as advocate and adversary are considered to be among the most important in the democratic scheme and probably are the chief reasons for the free-press guarantee of the First Amendment.

The press is frequently depicted as the fearless adversary of crime, of corruption and of oppressive government as well as of ill health, ill-made films, bad plays and poorly written books. The media is said to be the adversary of illiteracy, of improper nutrition, of radical rightist (or leftist) political activity, of unscrupulous merchants who prey on innocent consumers and of all evils virtually down to and including the man-eating shark. Or conversely, the press can be an advocate of any of these things that it may deem good rather than bad.

The First Amendment is often seen, however, as largely designed to protect the media in the performance of its duty as adversary of a powerful and autocratic government. And government has not always been content to serve as an unmoving, defenseless target for the media. Sometimes government strikes back—or strikes first. American history has had its full share of conflict between the press and the government. The past two decades, however, have witnessed combat between these old adversaries that at least equals any such contest in the two-century history of the United States. Many participants and observers say that during the Nixon Administration, government attempts to control the media exceeded those of any previous period.

In these two decades, television brought details of the blood-letting of an unpopular war into the living rooms of America. A Vice President spearheaded his government's attack on the media. Both this Vice President, Spiro T. Agnew, and later the President, Richard M. Nixon, were forced to resign under accusations of gross wrongdoing. In the case of the charges against the President, it was the media—or, more accurately, some members of the press—that brought the wrongdoing to light and pursued the Watergate scandal despite frantic efforts of influential men to cover it up. Members of the press established the White House's undeniable involvement in the wrongdoing and ultimately earned much of the credit for bringing down an erring President.

As the writings of Jefferson, Madison and other founders of the republic have already indicated, however, a free and independent press has long been expected to play an important part—in fact, a role akin to that of the government—in maintaining American freedoms. Justice Louis Brandeis of the Supreme Court is said to have alluded to this role in 1926 in his dissenting opinion in *Myers* v. *United States*. The purpose of the founders, he wrote, "was not to avoid friction but by means of the inevitable friction incident to the distribution of the government powers among three departments [or branches] to save the people from autocracy."

Supreme Court Justice Potter Stewart recalled Brandeis's remarks November 2, 1974 in an address at the Yale Law School Sesquicentennial Convocation. Stewart held that "the primary purpose of the constitutional guarantee of a free press was a similar one: to create a fourth institution outside the government as an additional check on the three official branches." Stewart cited the opening words of the Free Press Clause of the Massachusetts Constitution, drafted by John Adams: "The liberty of the press is essential to the security of the state."

Stewart noted how recent it was, "less than a decade ago, during the Vietnam years," that Americans became aware "of so-called investigative reporting and an adversary press—that is, a press adversary to the Executive Branch of the federal government. And only in the two short years that culminated . . . in the resignation of a President did we fully realize that enormous power that an investigative and adversary press can exert." Stewart rejected opinions that Nixon and Agnew "were hounded out of office by an arrogant and irresponsible press that had outrageously usurped dictatorial power. He likewise dismissed a more prevalent view that the organized press held "illegitimate power . . . in the political structure of our society."

"It is my thesis," Stewart declared, that ". . . the established American press in the past ten years, and particularly in the past two year [during which Agnew and Nixon submitted their forced resignations], has performed precisely the function it was intended to perform by those who wrote the First Amendment. . . ."

Stewart held that the Supreme Court's approach in recent cases involving the press "has uniformly reflected its understanding that the free-press guarantee is, in essence, a *structural* provision. . . . Most of the other provisions in the Bill of Rights protect specific liberties or specific rights of individuals: freedom of speech, freedom of worship, the right to counsel. . . . The publishing business is . . . the only organized private business that is given explicit constitutional protection."

Stewart rejected the suggestion "that freedom of the press means only that newspaper publishers are guaranteed freedom of expression." The free-speech clause already provided that. He pointed out that "between 1776 and the drafting of our Constitution, many of the state constitutions contained clauses protecting freedom of the press while . . . recognizing no general freedom of speech." He held that "by including both guarantees in the First Amendment, the founders quite clearly recognized the distinction between the two." Stewart also dismissed, among other opinions, the view that the guarantee's only purpose "is to insure that a newspaper will serve as a neutral forum for debate, a 'market place for idea.' " Instead, he asserted, the Constitution's purpose was to guarantee "the institutional autonomy of the press."

Recent libel decisions, Stewart indicated, confirm the institutional view of the organized press. Government officials "are, for all practical purposes, immune from libel and slander suits for statements that they make in the line of duty," he said. "This immunity . . . aims to insure bold and vigorous prosecution of the public's business. The same basic reasoning applies to the press. By contrast, the [Supreme] Court has never suggested that the constitutional right of free *speech* gives an individual any immunity from liability for either libel or slander."

Media Responsibility & 'Truth'

Taking into consideration both the rights and the functions of the press, is the media excessive in its attack on official wrongdoing? Is it thereby neglecting matters of greater national concern? And if it is at fault, does it have any "special responsibility" to police itself? The answer to all these questions appears to be "yes," said J. William Fulbright, a former chairman of the Senate Foreign Relations Committee, who discussed the issue at the National Press Club in Washington December 18, 1974.

During what Fulbright described as "the Vietnam and Watergate years," he conceded that the U.S. press had "demonstrated its commitment to the biblical injunction that 'the truth shall make you free.'" Fulbright, however, suggested that "an indiscriminate commitment to the truth" may obscure distinctions "between factual and philosophical truth, or between truth in the sense of factual disclosure and truth in the sense of insight." He expressed the opinion that "the latter . . . are higher forms of truth, more meaningful and also useful to society. . . ." Fulbright recalled the assertion of Voltaire that "there are truths which are not for all men, nor for all times." He added Mark Twain's advice that "truth is the most valuable thing we have. Let us economize it."

"In this Vietnam and Watergate decade," Fulbright said, "we have lost our ability to 'economize' the truth." America's "Puritan self-righteousness . . . has broken through the frail barriers of civility and restraint," he declared, "and the press has been in the vanguard of the new aggressiveness." While not advocating silence or suppression of criticism," Fulbright deplored "the shifting of the attack from policies to personalities, from matters of tangible consequence to the nation as a whole to matters of personal morality of uncertain relevance to the national interest."

"Since Watergate," Fulbright said, " . . . the media have acquired an undue preoccupation with the apprehension of wrongdoers, a fascination with the singer to the neglect of the song." He expressed doubt that "Watergate was as significant for the national interest as Mr. Nixon's extraordinary innovations in foreign policy," which "certainly took second place in the news to Watergate." "The press has exposed the wrongdoers most effectively," he agreed, "but I believe . . . you have neglected your higher responsibility of public education." Despite his disagreements with Lyndon B. Johnson over Vietnam and his resentment of Johnson's "deceit," Fulbright said he "never had the slightest sympathy with those who called President Johnson and his advisers 'war criminals.' "

"The media have a special responsibility for the restoration of civility in these matters," Fulbright declared, "not only because they have contributed to the incivility but also because there is no one to correct journalistic excesses except the members of the profession themselves. The media have become a fourth branch of government in every respect except for their immunity from checks and balances. . . . But because you cannot and should not be restrained from outside, you have a special responsibility to restrain yourselves."

It is not unusual for members of the press to admit to misgivings similar—but not always identical—to Fulbright's. Roscoe C. Born, vice editor of the *National Observer*, had done so in an address later excerpted in the August 3, 1974 edition of the *Observer*. The character of nearly every journalist has "a fundamental flaw," he said. This flaw "is an inborn desire to 'get' somebody," to print an article that gets somebody indicted, fired or defeated for election. Yet this urge is what drives journalists "to fulfill their role in our society," Born asserted. Otherwise there might be nobody to "expose evil so that society might correct it." This instinct to "get" somebody, however, might push a newsman into irresponsibility and unfairness, he warned. Journalists must examine their consciences "regularly," Born declared. They must be "more self-critical" and understand that abuse of the power of the press is as intolerable as abuse of government power.

Agnew Opens Nixon Administration War on Media

Spiro Theodore Agnew began his attack on the media November 13, 1969 with a speech before the Midwest Regional Republican Committee in Des Moines, Iowa. The Vice President acted as the Nixon Administration's spokesman in what was actually a wider offensive against domestic dissidence and criticism of United States conduct of the war in Vietnam.

The Des Moines speech was in reaction to commentary aired by the television networks November 3 immediately after a speech by President Richard M. Nixon on American policy in Vietnam. Agnew charged that most of the television commentators and guest experts were hostile to Nixon and his policy and had made up their minds about the issue even before they heard Nixon speak. Agnew's November 13 address, broadcast live throughout the country by all three major television networks, was the opening shot in a nearly four-year conflict between Agnew and the Nixon Administration on one side and the media on the other.

During this bitter controversy, Agnew and the Administration were accused of seeking to muzzle, repress, erode, harass, manipulate, coerce, supress, stifle or intimidate the media and even to destroy it as a free and independent entity. Agnew, Nixon and the Administration were accused of planning to nullify the First Amendment and possibly the whole Bill of Rights. They were described as the greatest menace to the free press in the history of the republic. Agnew and his supporters, of whom there were many, replied that his actions constituted nothing more than a fearless use of his right of free speech. He exercised this right, they held, to tell the truth as he saw it about a largely liberal, almost monolithic media establishment that misused its great power for sometimes un-American ends. The Agnew side denied any desire to harm press freedoms. It argued that its media adversary, with its alleged near monopoly of print and broadcast facilities, was damaging freedom by presenting only one side—the leftist side—of important issues that involved the freedom of the nation and, ultimately, the freedom of the world. Following Agnew's departure from government, documents became available that provided evidence of detailed planning within the Administration for a campaign of harsh pressure against the media. These plans counted on Agnew to play a prominent role in the anti-media campaign.

In his Des Moines salvo, Agnew discussed "the importance of the television news medium to the American people." "No medium has a more profound influence over public opinion," he said. "Nowhere in our system are there fewer checks on vast power. So, nowhere should there be more conscientious responsibility exercised than by the news media. . . ."

In regard to Nixon's November 3 speech, Agnew said it was "the most important address of his Administration, one of the most important of our decade." But "when the President completed his address—an address that he spent weeks in preparing," Agnew complained, "his words and policies were subjected to instant analysis and querulous criticism. . . . [Nixon's] audience of seventy million Americans . . . was inherited by a small band of network commentators and self-appointed analysts, the *majority* of whom expressed . . . their hostility to what he had to say."

"Every American has a right to disagree with the President . . . and to express publicity that disagreement," Agnew acknowledged. "But the President . . . has a right to communicate directly with the people who elected him," he continued, "and the people . . . have a right to make up their minds and form their own opinions about a Presidential address without having the President's words and thoughts characterized through the prejudices of hostile critics before they can even be digested."

"The purpose of my remarks," said Agnew, "is to focus your attention on this little group of men who not only enjoy a right of instant rebuttal to every Presidential address but, more importantly, wield a free hand in selecting, presenting and interpreting the great issues of our nation. . . . At least forty million Americans each night, it is estimated, watch the network news. Seven million of them view ABC, the remainder being divided between NBC and CBS. . . . For millions of Americans, the networks are the sole source of national and world news. In Will Rogers' observation, what you knew was what you read in the newspaper. Today, for growing millions of Americans, it is what they see and hear on their television sets."

Agnew suggested that prejudice and gross distortions were made possible by the way "this network news is determined": "A small group of men, numbering perhaps no more than a dozen 'anchormen,' commentators and executive producers, settle upon the twenty minutes or so of film and commentary that is to reach the public. This selection is made from the ninety to one hundred eighty minutes that may be available. Their powers of choice are broad. They decide what forty to fifty million Americans will learn of the day's events in the nation and the world. . . . These men can create national issues overnight. They can make or break . . . a moratorium on the war. They can elevate men from local obscurity to national prominence within a week. They can reward some politicians with national exposure and ignore others. For millions of Americans, the network reporter who covers a continuing issue . . . becomes, in effect, the presiding judge in a national trial by jury."

The networks, Agnew agreed, "have often used their power constructively and creatively to awaken the public conscience to critical problems. The networks made hunger and black-lung disease national issues overnight. The TV networks have done what no other medium could have done in terms of dramatizing the horrors of war. The networks have tackled our most difficult social problems with a directness and immediacy that is the gift of their medium. They have focused the nation's attention on its environmental abuses. . . ."

But the networks are also the power, Agnew said, "that elevated Stokely Carmichael and George Lincoln Rockwell from obscurity to national prominence. Nor is their power confined to the substantive. A raised eyebrow, an inflection of the voice, a caustic remark dropped in the middle of a broadcast can raise doubts in a million minds about the veracity of a public official or the wisdom of a government policy. One Federal Communications commissioner considers the power of the networks to equal that of local, state and federal government combined. Certainly, it represents a concentration of power over American public opinion unknown in history."

The men "who wield this power," said Agnew, "live and work in the geographical and intellectual confines of Washington, D.C. or New York City. . . . We can deduce that these men thus read the same newspapers and draw their political and social views from the same sources. Worse, they talk constantly to one another, thereby providing artificial reinforcement to their shared viewpoints."

Agnew quoted several TV news leaders on the question of whether their biases influence the selection and presentation of the news. According to David Brinkley, "Objectivity is impossible to normal human behavior"; newsmen, therefore, should strive for "fairness." An unnamed network anchorman was quoted as saying, "You can't expunge all your private convictions just because you sit in a seat like this and a camera starts to stare at you . . . I think your program has to reflect what your basic feelings are. I'll plead guilty to that." The latter newsman was cited by Agnew as charging that Nixon's "campaign commitments were no more durable than campaign balloons" and as accusing Nixon of having a "natural instinct to smash the enemy with a club or go after him with a meat ax." Such "slander," emanating "from the privileged sanctuary of a network studio . . ., had the apparent dignity of an objective statement," Agnew said.

"The American people would rightly not tolerate this kind of concentration of power in government," Agnew asserted. "Is it not fair and relevent to question its concentration in the hands of a tiny and closed fraternity of privileged men, elected by no one and enjoying a monopoly sanctioned and licensed by government? . . . As with other American institutions, perhaps it is time that the networks were made more responsive to the views of the nation and more responsible to the people they serve. I am not asking for government censorship or any other kind of censorship. I am asking whether a form of censorship already exists when the news that forty million Americans receive each night is determined by a handful of men responsible only to their corporate employers and filtered through a handful of commentators who admit to their own set of biases."

Agnew recalled Walter Lippman's decade-old assertion that "networks, which are few in number, have a virtual monopoly of a whole medium of communication." Lippmann had noted "an essential and radical difference between television and printing. . . . The three or four competing television stations control virtually all that can be received over the air by ordinary television sets. But, besides the mass circulation dailies, there are the weeklies, the monthlies, the out-of-town newspapers and books. If a man does not like his newspaper, he can read another from out of town, or wait for a weekly news magazine. It is not ideal. But it is infinitely better than the situation in television. There, if a man does not like what the networks offer him, all he can do is turn them off and listen to a phonograph."

Replies to Agnew's attacks were made by the presidents of all three major television networks the same day that Agnew made his speech.

Julian Goodman of NBC (the National Broadcasting Co.) charged that Agnew's "attack on television news is an appeal to prejudice" and use of high office "to criticize the way a government-licensed news medium covers the activities of government itself." Goodman suggested that Agnew "would prefer a different kind of television reporting—one that would be subservient to whatever political group was in authority at the time."

Leonard H. Goldenson of ABC (American Broadcasting Companies) defended ABC news as "fair and objective." He said his network would "continue to report the news accurately and fully, confident in the ultimate judgment of the American public."

Dr. Frank Stanton of CBS (Columbia Broadcasting System) called Agnew's speech an "unprecedented attempt by the Vice President of the United States to intimidate a news medium which depends for its existence upon government licenses." Whatever the deficiencies of CBS newsmen, Stanton said, "they are minor compared to those of a press which would be subservient to the executive power of government."

Stanton extended his reply to Agnew November 25 in a radio broadcast before the International Radio & Television Society in New York. He reiterated his charges that Agnew was trying to intimidate the networks. "If these threats implicit in the developments of the past week are not openly recognized, unequivocally denounced and firmly resisted," he warned, "freedom of communications in this country will suffer a setback that will not be limited to checking the freedom of television or barring critical comment on government policy. It will precipitate an erosion that will inevitably destroy the most powerful safeguard of a free society—free, unhampered and unharassed news media." Stanton conceded that broadcast journalism was not beyond criticism. "We are *not* unaccountable," he said. "We are *not* clandestine. We have *no* end product that is not seen and judged by everyone. But such open criticism is a far cry from sharp reminders from high official quarters that we are licensed or that if we don't examine ourselves, we in common with other media 'invite' the government to move in."

The chairman of the Federal Communications Commission (FCC), Dean Burch, had said November 14 that he did not consider Agnew's remarks intimidating. "Had the Vice President suggested that the government censor these networks, that would have been another thing entirely," he declared. Instead, as Burch saw it, Agnew was urging the networks to "examine themselves to see whether they were doing a good job." He said he considered Agnew's speech to be "thoughtful, provocative" and worthy of "careful consideration by the industry and the public. Burch was reported to have said that he had received complaints about the "instant analysis" after Nixon's November 3 speech.

Nicholas Johnson, one of the FCC commissioners, said November 17, however, that the Agnew speech had "frightened network executives and newsmen in ways that may cause serious and permanent harm to independent journalism and free speech in America." While "a handful of men" did "control what the American people see through their television screens," Johnson said, the answer was "not to transfer this power from a handful of men in New York to a handful of men in the White House."

Clark R. Mollenhoff, then special counsel to President Nixon, said November 15 that Agnew's speech "reflected the views of the Administration." Herbert G. Klein, Nixon's director of communications, indicated to interviewers on CBS's "Face the Nation" program November 16 that a failure of the media to correct itself might be considered an invitation to government action. He said Agnew's speech mirrored a widely held view in top Administration levels. "I think you can go beyond that," he said. "All of the news media needs to reexamine itself in the format it has, and its approach to problems of news, to meet the current issues of the day." Klein included "the newspapers very thoroughly in this, as well as the networks. If you look at the problems you have today and you fail to continue to examine them, you do invite the government to come in. I would not like to see that happen."

White House Press Secretary Ronald L. Ziegler said November 15 that Nixon had not discussed Agnew's speech with the Vice President. Ziegler November 17 defended the views expressed by Agnew and Klein on the media issue. He emphasized that the Nixon Administration had "absolutely no desire" to censor the news.

Agnew found at least a partial supporter in a major television newsman. Howard K. Smith, anchorman in Washington for ABC's main news show, said November 19, "I agree with some of what Mr. Agnew said. In fact, I said some of it before he did."

The Agnew address, however, was widely denounced by other media representatives, Democratic leaders and civil liberties supporters. James Day, president of National Educational Television, charged November 13 that Agnew's "sweeping remarks . . . both misrepresent and misinterpret the news function of television." Thomas P. Hoving, chairman of the National Citizens

Committee for Broadcasting, said the same day that Agnew's "disgraceful attack . . . officially leads us as a nation into an ugly era of the most fearsome suppression and intimidation. Senator Edward M. Kennedy of Massachusetts, then the Senate Democratic whip, asserted November 14 that "we are now witnessing an attack designed to pit American against American—an attack with the ultimate aim of dividing this country into those who support and those who do not support our President's position on Vietnam." The American Civil Liberties Union said November 15 that Agnew had voiced a "clear and chilling threat" of censorship.

Agnew Expands Campaign Against Media

Exactly one week after his Des Moines speech, Agnew extended his criticism of the media by including newspapers and magazines among his targets. Speaking in Montgomery, Ala. November 20, 1969 before the city Chamber of Commerce, Agnew described many of the answers to his earlier address as "classic examples of overreaction." He insisted that "I am opposed to censorship of television or the press in any form. I don't care whether censorship is imposed by government or whether it results from management in the choice and presentation of the news by a little fraternity having similar social and political views. I am against censorship in all forms."

Agnew asserted, however, that "a broader spectrum of national opinion *should* be represented among the commentators of the network news. Men who can articulate other points of view *should* be brought forward. And a high wall of separation *should* be raised between what is news and what is commentary. And the American people *should* be made aware of the trend toward the monopolization of the great public information vehicles and the concentration of more and more power over public opinion in fewer and fewer hands."

Agnew noted that "a single company, in the nation's capital, holds control of the largest newspaper in Washington, D.C., *and* one of the four major television stations, *and* an all-news radio station, *and* one of the three major news magazines—all grinding out the same editorial line—and this is not a subject you have seen debated on the editorial pages of the *Washington Post* or *The New York Times*." Agnew added that "I am not recommending the dismemberment of the Washington Post Co. I am merely pointing out that the public should be aware that these four voices harken to the same master."

Agnew lamented the deaths of a great number of newspapers in the cities of America. "Lacking the vigor of competition, some of those that have survived have . . . grown fat and irresponsible," he declared. "I offer an example: When 300 Congressmen and 59 Senators signed a letter endorsing the President's policy in Vietnam, it was news. . . . Even the *Washington Post* and the *Baltimore Sun*—scarcely house organs of the Nixon Administration—placed it on the front page. . . . The next morning *The New York Times*, which considers itself America's paper of record, did not carry a word. . . . [Yet] if a theology student in Iowa should get up at a PTA luncheon in Sioux City and attack the President's Vietnam policy, my guess is that you would probably find it reported somewhere the next morning in *The New York Times*. . . ."

Agnew suggested that much of what the media said about Vietnam, campus dissent and other important issues was wrong. He considered it "my right and duty to stand up and speak out for the values in which I believe," Agnew indicated, and as a result was sometimes characterized as "a bigot, a racist or a fool." "I am not asking any immunity from criticism," he said. "But my political and journalistic adversaries sometimes seem to be asking . . . that I circumscribe my rhetorical freedom while they place no restrictions on theirs. . . . We do not accept those terms for continuing the national dialogue. The day when the network commentators and even gentlemen of *The New York Times* enjoyed a form of diplomatic immunity from comment and criticism of what they said—that day is past. . . . When they go beyond fair comment and criticism, they will be called upon to defend their statements and their positions just as we must defend ours. . . . I do not seek to intimidate the press, the networks or anyone else from speaking out. But the time for blind acceptance of their opinions is gone. And the time for naive belief in their neutrality is gone. . . ."

Both the *Times* and the *Washington Post* replied the same day to Agnew's criticism. Arthur Ochs Sulzberger, president and publisher of the *Times*, denied that his paper "ever sought or enjoyed immunity from comment and criticism." He called some of Agnew's statements inaccurate. The item on Congressional support for Vietnam policy was printed in the *Times*, Sulzberger asserted, although, "unfortunately," not in the Washington edition (an early edition). Sulzberger asserted that there was no editorial significance in carrying a story on Page 11 rather than on Page 3.

Mrs. Katharine Graham, president of the Washington Post Company, said Agnew's remarks about her firm were "not supported by the facts." Each Post branch "operated autonomously," and the branches competed "vigorously with one another," she declared.

President Nixon said at his news conference December 2 that Agnew had "rendered a public service in talking in a very dignified and courageous way about a problem that many Americans are concerned about . . . the coverage by news media . . . of public figures." According to Nixon, Agnew "advocated that there should be free expression" and "recognized—as I do—that there should be opinion." Perhaps Agnew's point "should be well taken," said Nixon, that television "might well follow the practice of newspapers of separating news from opinion." He considered these "useful suggestions," Nixon said. "Perhaps the networks disagreed with the criticism, but I would suggest that they should be just as dignified and just as reasonable in answering the criticism as he was in making them."

A third major speech criticizing the media was made by Agnew May 22, 1970 at a Republican fund-raising dinner in Houston, Tex. He denounced "the liberal news media of this country, those really illiberal, self-appointed guardians of our destiny who would like to run the country without ever submitting to the elective process as we in public office must do."

Agnew specifically attacked the editorial writers of *The New York Times*, the *Washington Post*, the *Atlanta Constitution*, the *New Republic* and *I. F. Stone's Bi-Weekly*. He denounced *Washington Post* cartoonist Herblock, syndicated columnist Carl T. Rowan and columnists Anthony Lewis, James Reston and Tom Wicker of *The New York Times*, Hugh Sidey of *Life* magazine and Pete Hamill and Harriet Van Horne of the *New York Post*.

Despite complaints about Vice Presidential rhetoric, the loudest of which came from "the columns and editorials of the liberal news media," Agnew said, President Nixon "has refused to curb my statements on behalf of this Administration's policies, or to tell me what words to use or what tone to take in my speeches. And . . . I have refused to 'cool it' . . . until those self-righteous lower their voices. . . . There is too much at stake in the nation for us to leave the entire field of public commentary to them."

Agnew charged that some of the press "pundits make my rhetoric seem tame." He quoted such terms used against Nixon, himself and Nixon policy as "erratic," "irrational," "deception," "demagoguery," "chauvinism," "descent to gutter fighting," "maudlin," "crafty," "fraud" and "transparently phony."

Agnew charged that Rowan, Herblock "and others" had suggested "that I had something to do with the deaths" of four Kent State University students, who were shot by National Guardsmen during a protest. "But the most vicious attempt to transfer the blame for the Kent State student deaths that I have read was . . . by columnist Pete Hamill," Agnew said. "Listen to his irrational raving: 'When you call campus dissenters 'bums,' as Nixon did . . ., you should not be surprised when they are shot . . . by National Guardsmen. . . . At Kent State, two boys and two girls were shot to death by men unleashed by a President's slovenly rhetoric.' . . ."

"This goes on daily in the editorial pages of some very large, very reputable newspapers in this country—not all of them in the East," Agnew said. "And it pours out of the television set and the radio in a daily torrent. . . . 'But you are the Vice President,' they say to me. 'You should choose your language more carefully.' Nonsense. I have sworn I will uphold the Constitution against all enemies, foreign and domestic. Those who would tear our country apart or try to bring down its government are enemies. . . . I have an obligation to all the people of the United States to call things as I see them. . . . Nothing would be more pleasing to some of the editors and columnists I have quoted . . . than to have me simply shut up and disappear. . . .

"Finally a word about . . . the electronic news media. I have tried tonight to be *specific* in my criticism. I realize I have left out many who are in the business of second-guessing the President and who should have been included. I hope we can get around to them later. But I also recognize there are many others in the news profession—a group upon whom the country has to depend for an *honest* report of what is going on in this world—and that they are attempting to live up to this responsibility, most of them successfully. I exclude them totally from the criticism I make here. And I compliment them for doing their jobs well under strong counter-pressures, often within their own offices and among less responsible colleagues.

"It does bother me, however, that the press—as a group—

regards the First Amendment as its own private preserve. Every time I criticize what I consider to be excesses or faults in the news business, I am accused of repression, and the leaders of the various media professional groups wave the First Amendment as they denounce me. That happens to be *my* amendment too. It guarantees *my* free speech as much as it does their freedom of the press. So I hope that will be remembered the next time a 'muzzle Agnew' campaign is launched. There is room for all of us—and for our divergent views—under the First Amendment."

Addressing the International Federation of Newspaper Publishers in Washington June 5, 1970, Agnew upheld the principle of freedom of the press. His differences with "some of the news media," he said, had arisen not over their right to criticize government or public officials but my right to criticize them." Agnew accused the news media in general of not "telling both sides of the story." He particularly objected to the media's coverage of the war in Vietnam. He described the war reporting as "slanted against American involvement . . . without any attempt at balance."

Agnew said June 1, 1971 that his criticisms of the media over the past year and a half added up to no more that a "call on the free press of this country . . . to police itself against excesses that on occasion have been so blatant that they have undermined the confidence of the public in the credibility of the news media as well as the credibility of the government." Speaking to radio station owners affiliated with the Mutual Broadcasting System, who were meeting in the Bahamas, Agnew said that the media had reacted to this "constructive" criticism, offered by him and others, with a "frenzy about intimidation and repression." He warned that "attempts to portray the government as anxious to control or suppress the news media" would "backfire" and compound the "credibility problem" faced by the media.

Media coverage of the September 1971 revolt of inmates at the state prison in Attica, N.Y. was attacked by Agnew September 27. Thirty-two prisoners and ten guards, the latter hostages, were killed in the prisoner insurrection and its suppression. Agnew's comment was made at a meeting of the International Association of Chiefs of Police in Anaheim, Calif.

Agnew accused the radical Left and the news media of trying to make Attica "another *cause celebre* in the pantheon of radical revolutionary propaganda." He said that instead of paying tribute to six hundred thirty-three law officers killed in the United States in the previous decade, "inordinate attention" had been "focused on the self-declared and proven enemies of our society." Agnew denied that the need for penal reform was the issue at Attica. "Only by the total inversion of all civilized values can those among the militant inmates which killed a guard and slashed the throats of fellow inmates during the period of their holdout be termed heroes in a struggle for human life and dignity," he declared. He assailed the media for giving wide currency to "the most inflammatory and baseless charges" of convicted criminals and their sympathizers.

'The Selling of the Pentagon'

Agnew, other Nixon Administration officials and several Congress members became embroiled in 1971 in controversy with the Columbia Broadcasting System over alleged inaccuracies, distortions or even outright falsifications in a CBS television documentary criticizing the Pentagon's expensive program of publicity on behalf of the military establishment. The dispute is worth examining in some detail because of the wide antagonisms it created, because it illustrates several aspects of the adversary relationship between the media and the government and because it involves examples of allegedly deceptive television treatment and explains how such practices can lead to further false interpretations of what has been televised.

The program, entitled "The Selling of the Pentagon," was written and produced by Peter Davis. It was first shown February 23, 1971 and was rebroadcast February 27. According to the documentary, the Pentagon spent nearly $30 million a year to enhance its image among Americans by staging elaborate war games, circulating propaganda films and sending out officers in uniform to warn about the menace of communism. In his summing up, Roger Mudd, the narrator, said that "on this broadcast we have seen violence made glamorous, expensive weapons advertised as if they were automobiles, biased opinions presented as straight facts. Defending the country not just with arms but also with ideology, Pentagon propaganda insists on America's role as the cop on every beat in the world."

Following the first broadcast, the program was lauded by television critic Jack Gould in *The New York Times* February 24 as "brilliant." He said that in the documentary, "CBS nailed down ... the chairman of the House Armed Services Committee making a propaganda film for the Department of Defense, ..." and CBS News President Richard S. Salant "struck a whale of a constructive blow for unfettered TV journalism free from Washington manipulation."

William C. Woods asserted in the *Washington Post* that the program "belongs to the finest tradition of muckraking TV documentary." "Taken as a whole," he declared, "it amounts to a gutsy and intelligent show. . . ." Woods reported that the documentary relied "strongly on a series of speeches given by Senator J. William Fulbright on December 1, 2, 4 and 5, 1969, which were entered in the *Congressional Record* [and] later worked into his book *The Pentagon Propaganda Machine*." (The book was published in November 1970.)

After seeing a special Capitol Hill screening of the CBS documentary, Representative F. Edward Hébert (Democrat of Louisiana), chairman of the House Armed Services Committee, denounced the documentary February 26 as a "vicious piece of propaganda." At one point in his criticism of the program, Hébert said that "all I ask is accuracy," and CBS's Salant replied, "My only comment is: 'He got it.' "

Among his criticism, Hébert discussed a portion of the documentary showing his interviewing Major James Rowe, a Green Beret who had been a prisoner of war in Vietnam. Hébert acknowledged that his office had given the video tape to CBS News but said he had been led to believe that it was to be used for a CBS documentary on prisoners of war. A CBS official denied that CBS had made such a commitment. He said that in July 1970 CBS had asked Hébert's office for use of the film for a documentary on "how the Pentagon presents its message to the American people." According to this CBS spokesman, Hébert's office gave CBS permission to use the film or any part of it.

Hébert March 3 inserted in the *Congressional Record* a memo dated February 26, 1971 from his press aide, Lou Gehrig Burnett. Burnett told Hébert in the memo: "James Branon of CBS . . . called me . . . and said that his network was planning to do a documentary on the POW [prisoner of war] situation. He was seeking any film we might have in which you interviewed an ex-POW. Branon said the documentary would explore the plight of the POW and his family. . . . [A]fter checking with you, we obtained a video tape of the interview . . . with Major James Rowe. I . . . mailed it to CBS. Branon called me several more times. . . . I obtained for him the names of every Congressman who had ever done a TV or radio interview with an ex-POW. . . . [H]e again said the video tape would be used for a POW special on CBS. Later, after he had obtained the video tape from us, he called to say . . . that he didn't think he could use any of it. . . . Branon had asked for the names of representatives of the various branches of service with whom he could discuss POW publicity. I gave him the names of the directors of the liaison offices . . . of the Army, Air Force and Navy. Later, . . . [Branon] said they were having difficulties [with the documentary] and he didn't know if they would be able to do it."

Hébert said in his March 3 statement that "I, in no way, assume that the news media is out of bounds by criticizing the Pentagon. As a former newspaper editor, I know that no segment of the government is, or should be, free from severe criticism by the news media. . . . But presentations which are biased throughout, which are slanted to only use language and items which support that bias, and which clearly make false innuendos about individuals in order to prove the bias—such presentations detract from the media's function of being a true critic of society and make it more difficult for the worthwhile criticism to be presented and accepted."

In "The Selling of the Pentagon," Hébert noted, "the commentator at one point begins as follows: 'Using sympathetic Congressmen, the Pentagon tries to counter what it regards as the antimilitary tilt of network reporting. War heroes are made available for the taped home district TV reports from pro-Pentagon politicians. Here Representative F. Edward Hébert . . . asks Major James Rowe . . . what keeps the Viet Cong fighting.' "

Hébert held that "anyone seeing that on TV . . . is given several clear inferences which were obviously intended by the program: First, that the Pentagon 'used' Hébert for the program because he was sympathetic. [Hébert described himself as actually a stern critic of the military.] Second, that, therefore, the program was the Pentagon's idea. Third, that the program was planned by the Pentagon to counter network TV reporting. Fourth, that Major Rowe was supplied to me by the Pentagon." "All of these allegations are pure falsehoods," Hébert declared. As an indication of "how these inferences carry over to the people who should know better," Hébert said that "one news reporter was so misled as to write in his paper: 'The film footage shows Hébert in an Army-produced film interviewing a Green Beret officer who had been a prisoner of war." Thus, according to Hébert, "the false inferences of the original program can lead to flatly stated falsehoods"—such as the newspaper article saying "flat out that the film was an Army-produced film." Hébert called this "the ripple effect of false innuendoes." He added that "the reporter in this case was kind enough to call me and subsequently admit the error and printed a correction in his paper."

In the April 1971 edition of *Air Force* magazine, Senior Editor Claude Witze discussed alleged inaccuracies, distortions and misleading practices he said he had detected in the documentary. (Witze's comments were made public March 15.)

In a sequence showing a lecture by Marine Colonel John A. MacNeil, five sentences "came from four different spots on the camera record, and the sequence was rearranged," Witze reported. The rearrangement gave the sentences MacNeil spoke a meaning different from MacNeil's original meaning, Witze wrote. Part of what MacNeil said was a direct quotation from Laotian Prime Minister Souvanna Phouma, but the attribution was deleted. "CBS distorted the film to make its viewers think Colonel MacNeil said" what actually had been said by Souvanna Phouma, Witze charged. The words were rearranged by CBS "to make . . . [MacNeil's] presentation sound inept, stupid, wrong, vicious," according to Witze.

Witze cited an instance in which Assistant Defense Secretary (for Public Affairs) Daniel Z. Henkin answered interviewer Roger Mudd's question about the purpose of public displays of military equipment. If Henkin's reply, as broadcast, "was a bit disjointed and . . . did not answer the question," Witze said, the reason was that most of what was used had been taken from another part of the Henkin interview.

In a March 4 letter answering questions posed by Representative Hébert, Henkin had documented the assertion that his responses to Mudd's questions were "sometimes transposed to questions other than the one to which . . . [he had] responded." "Some answers were taken out of context by cutting the rearrangement," Henkin said. As an example, Mudd had asked whether "the sort of information about the drug problem you [the military] have and racial problem you have and the budget problems you have—is that the sort of information that gets passed out at state fairs by sergeants who are standing next to rockets?" The Henkin reply, as broadcast, was: "No, I wouldn't limit that to sergeants standing next to any kind of exhibit. Now, there are those who contend that this is propaganda. I do not agree with this." According to Henkin's documentation (a transcript of the unedited interview), the last two sentences "were lifted from the middle of an earlier question" and "referred to data on increasing Soviet threat." Sentences in which Henkin actually answered Mudd's question were not used.

Agnew entered the controversy March 18, calling the documentary a "subtle but vicious broadside against the nation's defense establishment." Addressing the Middlesex Republican Club in Boston, Agnew questioned the credibility of the program. Agnew said that two CBS newsmen who produced the film had also worked on other documentaries that used questionable editing and production techniques. CBS was also attacked by Senator Robert Dole (Republican of Kansas), who accused it and the other two national television networks March 19 of biased news coverage. Dole, chairman of the Republican National Committee, said the news coverage of the National Broadcasting Company (NBC) and the American Broadcasting Companies (ABC) was also prejudiced, but he said CBS was most guilty of biased reporting. Agnew said March 20 that CBS had not responded to his March 18 speech, and he challenged the network to admit or deny his charges "of error and propagandistic manipulation" in the Pentagon documentary and others.

CBS rebroadcast the documentary March 23. It followed the documentary with an edited version of the criticism by Agnew, Defense Secretary Melvin R. Laird and Representative Hébert and a defense of the film by CBS News President Salant. Hébert called the film "one of the most un-American things I've ever seen . . . on the tube." Laird said he thought "there probably could have been a little more professionalism shown in putting the show together." Salant said that "no one has refuted the essential accuracy" of the documentary.

Agnew renewed his criticism of CBS March 24, charging the network with "Deliberately publishing untruths." In an interview in St. Louis, the Vice President said he was "totally dissatisfied with what the network characterized as a rebuttal on the part of Administration officials, including myself," following the March

23 rebroadcast. He accused CBS of editing his earlier remarks and comments of Laird and Hebert and of having "showed the ones they wanted to show."

The attitude of the press seemed largely to be agreement that misrepresentation in a documentary deserved critism but that Agnew's denunciation of CBS was excessive and perhaps verged on the threatening. *The Boston Globe* suggested that there was no serious misrepresentation in the fact that the rearrangement of film sequences had made it appear that Colonel MacNeil was using his own words when he actually was quoting Souvanna Phouma. According to a *Globe* editorial March 20, "it struck us that it didn't matter much who said it, the colonel or Souvanna Phouma or Mr. Eisenhower—they all believed it, didn't they?" *The Providence* (R.I.) *Journal,* on the contrary, said editorially March 24 that if CBS's "employees distorted reality to make a sharper case, as Mr. Witze has charged without challenge, then CBS did more to cast a shadow on its own credibility as a producer of documentaries that did Mr. Agnew."

According to an *Arizona Republic* editorial March 22, "network documentaries are not usually as crude as the hatchet job done on the Pentagon, where scenes were spliced, edited, and chopped beyond recognition in order to make the worst possible case against the 'military establishment.' Most often the documentaries [of all three networks] are simply unbalanced: They set out to present a liberal point of view, and film clips and interviews are carefully selected and arranged so that viewers are left with the desired impression."

Commenting on the media's response to the criticism of the documentary—and particularly the response of the broadcast media—the Portland *Oregonian* said editorially March 23 that "the electronic media is understandably more sensitive than the print newsmen, as it operates at sufferance of the government, and has not been in the news business long enough to develop the thick skins of newspapers that have grown up under a constant bombardment of criticism, both fair and unfair, but protected by the First Amendment. Further, television news has come out of the traditions of show business. It judges news by whether it has filmed it or not, and then it must look for the most exciting and entertaining film clips for its nightly show that must compete for audience ratings or go under."

The *St. Louis Post-Dispatch* speculated editorially March 25 that Agnew's purpose in "resuming his attack on the news media" was to ensure his retention on the ticket in the next election. The *Post-Dispatch* suggested that "CBS and other news media would do well to comprehend the political motives of the performance and to take a bit of Mr. Agnew's own advice by not getting uptight about it. The television networks have nothing to apologize for when they perform the function of an independent press which declines to regard itself as an agency of the government."

"The controversy over 'The Selling of the Pentagon,'" said *The San Diego Union* March 26, "leads us to the conclusion that the Defense Department can well afford to re-examine some of its informational programs—and CBS can well afford to re-examine its own credibility." By employing "a sleight-of-hand with film and sound" and because of other "departures from good journalism," the *Union* said, "what CBS intended to be an indictment of armed forces public relations emerges more as an indictment of its own standards."

Editorial comment by *The Washington Post* March 26 provoked a reply by CBS News President Salant and a minicontroversy between CBS and the *Post*.

In its editorial, the *Post* characterized the documentary as "a highly valuable and informative exposition of a subject about which the American people should know more—not less." It added that "some of the criticism of the documentary—in terms of production techniques and occasional inaccuracies—is valid...." The editorial said that "the line between reporting and staging events in this kind of television program is a fine one and also one that is too easily crossed.... And we think this line is crossed when taped interviews are edited in such a way as to alter the actual response of those of whom questions are asked. Such was the case... in the responses—as they were given and as they appeared—of Assistant Secretary of Defense Daniel Z. Henkin." The reasons given for this practice do not make it "acceptable," the *Post* declared. Failure to preserve sequence, indicate cuts "and/or give the subject of the interview an opportunity to see and approve his revised or altered remarks," the editorial continued, "does in fact result in a material distortion of the record, especially when the viewer is under the impression that what he is watching is what actually and exactly occurred."

Salant's reply, printed in the March 30 issue of the *Post*, described the editorial as "obviously written by one who has long labored on the editorial page—and one on the news pages." He said: The editing of a news or documentary broadcast "is precisely as important as, and possibly no more complicated than . . . editing in the print medium . . . —the process by which any journalist rejects or accepts, selects and omits, and almost always compresses material available to him." The *Post* does "not question the right, indeed the professional obligation of your reporters to do this," Salant wrote, nor of the editors who received the reporter's finished story to continue the editing. "But you question not only our right to do the same thing," Salant charged, "but also the methods by which we edit, and even our motives. . . . [You] suggest, indeed recommend, that our rules should be different than your rules, that sound journalistic ethics and the First Amendment are somehow divisible between rights granted to journalists whose work comes out in ink and somewhat lesser rights for journalists whose work comes out electronically."

"But most astonishing of all," Salant continued, *"you propose that we should give the subject of the interview an opportunity to see and approve his revised remarks. . . .* You know . . . that this strikes at the very core of independent and free journalism. To grant a subject such a right of review is to remove the basic journalistic function of editing from the hands of the journalist and place it—in the case of the documentary in question—in the hands of the Pentagon. . . . We are all after the same thing: to be fair, to inform the public fairly and honestly. . . . I submit that we are as careful about editing, as concerned with what is fair and proper and in balance, as rigorous in our internal screening and editorial control processes as any journalistic organization. . . . We believe . . . that 'The Selling of the Pentagon' was edited fairly and honestly. . . ."

The *Post* March 30 also printed its reply to Salant's letter. It said Salant "invests the term 'editing' with functions and freedoms well beyond anything we regard as common or acceptable practice." The editorial denied recommending a double standard for editing—separate rules for print and electronic media. "We were and are objecting to the fact that *specifically, in relation to question-and-answer sequences,* two sets of standards *already* exist," the *Post* said," and that what he and others in television appear to regard as simple 'editing' seems to us to take an excess of unacknowledged liberties with the direct quotations of the principals involved. . . ."

What the *Post* said it disapproved is "the practice of printing highly rearranged material in a Q-and-A sequence as if it were verbatim text, without indicating to the reader that changes had been made and/or without giving the subject an opportunity to approve revisions in the original exchange. It is . . . presenting as a direct six-sentence quotation from a colonel, a 'statement' composed of a first sentence from page 55 of his prepared text, followed by a second sentence from page 36, followed by a third and fourth from page 48, and a fifth from page 73, and a sixth from page 88. . . . [T]his type of procedure is 1) not 'editing' in any conventional sense and 2) likely to undermine both the broadcast's credibility and public confidence in that credibility. . . . 'The Selling of the Pentagon' presented this statement as if it were one that had actually been made—verbatim—by the colonel; TV can and does simulate an impression of actuality in the way it conveys such rearranged material. . . ."

The *Post* editorial also cited the radical rearrangement of Henkin's answers. It said: "Surely, something different from and less cosmic than a challenge to CBS's First Amendment rights is involved in the question of whether or not the subject of such a rearranged interview should not be given a chance to see and approve what he will be demonstrated to have said. . . ."

As the controversy continued, the *Post* printed letters from NBC News President Reuven Frank and from Fred W. Friendly, the Edward R. Murrow professor of broadcast journalism at Columbia University. It also printed an amplification of its own views.

Frank, in his letter, criticized the *Post* for what he described as suggestions "that when television news uses excerpts of a speech or statement, it explains how such excerpting was done" and that "we ask the speaker to approve this use of some of his remarks, since we are not using all of them." He said that in "television news film, as in print, such remarks are excerpted from importance from material of less importance, for interest from material of varying interest, for time because unlimited time, like unlimited space, is not available. . . . To deny any reporter or editor not only the right but the responsibility of choosing which sentences in any public statement are interesting or important is to deny that reporters or editors are needed. . . . It is frightening to think that the lead editorial in an important American newspaper should suggest that widely circulated news reports in another medium should delegate this choosing process to the most narrowly interested party, the man who made the speech."

Friendly called it "curious" that the *Post* "should choose to overlook the common bond between good broadcasting and . . . good newspapering—fair and honorable editing." He assailed what he indicated was an implication "that a double standard should exist—one for newspapers and one for broadcast." Friendly described his "understanding that one of the major points of newspaper independence has been never to permit a news source to review and/or edit what is to appear in the newspaper. . . . [T]his protection of editorial independence is still a benchmark of broadcast news." According to Friendly, "the strongest motivation of a news producer or editor is to preserve original meaning. . . . Implicitly, in a question and answer sequence, the original context must be preserved."

"I do not mean to imply that 'The Selling of the Pentagon' was without its imperfections," Friendly wrote. "I have spent some time and had considerable correspondence with its producers and its detractors. In every discussion and in every letter, it has become clear that the imperfections do not mar the central thrust of the broadcast, *i.e.,* that '. . . this gigantic and colossal propaganda machine on the banks of the Potomac . . . is still turned on,' as Congressman F. Edward Hébert once put it. We need more such documentaries, not fewer. . . . By equating film and tape editing with staging, I fear that your editorial tends to cloud the fundamental issue. It is akin to the Vice President charging that your reporters' copy is being distorted by your editors. . . ."

In its reply, the *Post* expressed apparent surprise that Frank and Friendly as well as Salant "seem to think that we are proposing to surrender up some sacred journalistic right; that we are disinterested in the 'protection of editorial independence' . . . [or] proposing to 'deny any reporter or editor not only the right but the responsibility of choosing which sentences in any public statement are interesting or important'. . . ." The *Post* said that "we were not even talking about public statements or speeches, and still less . . . about newscasts or news stories—the run of the mill news fare. Both media . . . reserve the right to exercise their own judgments about what to use and what to ignore, what to play up or down, how to paraphrase. And both are equally subject to errors of judgment in compressing material into limited time or space. . . . There is no issue of 'delegating the choosing process' here." The issue, the *Post* held, was that of arbitrarily rearranging the "Qs" and "As" in question-and-answer interviews "so as to destroy or distort their original relationship—to present as the 'A' something that didn't in fact arise from the original 'Q.' " When the print media edits transcripts of Qs and As, the *Post* said, it indicates the change to the reader "by dots or asterisks." The innovative television industry could surely "figure out an easy way to identify disjointed excerpts as such," the *Post* declared. "Nor does it seem to us to be too large a surrender of rights, when there has been a serious rearrangement of the original material, to allow the subject to at least look at the product before it is printed or aired and to argue about it; we offered this as an option . . . in special cases, on the theory that if the subject doesn't recognize or accept the validity of what he is represented as having said, it has no validity."

The *Post* noted that its above response appeared under its "F.Y.I." heading, a rubric it used for "examining our own performances and practices" and for printing regular "commentary on the news business." "We do it," the *Post* said, "because we believe there has been a long-developing deterioration of public trust in the news media—as in other institutions—and that the way to deal with this is not to stand aloof but to talk about it; to deal with our business as we treat everybody else's business; to be a little less arrogant about conceding the bare possibility of a mistake every once in a while. . . ."

The House Interstate & Foreign Commerce Committee April 8 served a subpoena directing CBS to turn over for investigation all televised and untelevised materials that were used to produce "The Selling of the Pentagon." Representative Harley O. Staggers (Democrat of West Virginia), chairman of the Commerce Committee and its Special Subcommittee on Investigations, which served the order, said the sensible course in the controversy was "to get the facts." Dr. Frank Stanton, president of CBS, said the network would make available only the materials that had actually been broadcast.

CBS refused April 20 to comply with the Congressional subpoena. Although it did furnish the subcommittee with the file and transcript of the program as it appeared on television, CBS did not turn over the demanded "outtakes," portions of film edited out before the broadcast. In a letter to Staggers, CBS said again April 30 that it would not turn over all the materials collected for the documentary. CBS said that "compliance with the subpoena would have a chilling effect on the ability of journalists at CBS and throughout the profession to report and interpret the news— including, of course, the conduct of government officials."

The subcommittee May 26 issued a new subpoena, demanding the appearance of the CBS president (Stanton) and directing that CBS make available key materials used to make the film. The new subpoena replaced the earlier one.

White House Communications Director Herbert Klein said in a speech in Des Moines May 26 that the Nixon Administration did not back the subcommittee's investigation of the documentary. He said of the investigation: "I believe this is wrong and an infringement on freedom of the press. It could lead to further subpoenas of a reporter's notes." Klein added that the president was not "in favor of further restrictions" on communications media.

Daniel Z. Henkin, assistant secretary of defense for public affairs, had criticized CBS May 12 for what he described as misrepresentations in "The Selling of the Pentagon," but he defended the network's right to produce a program critical of the Defense Department's public relations activities. In testimony before the Special Subcommittee on Investigations, Henkin said: "The Pentagon is not for sale, and not for sale either is the right of a free press to criticize the Pentagon."

Stanton June 24 again refused to give the subcommittee all the materials used to produce the documentary. He told the subcommittee that his refusal was based on the First Amendment's freedom-of-the-press privileges. He contended that the vitality of television journalism needed the same freedom from government "surveillance" as that accorded newspapers. The board of directors of the National Association of Broadcasters June 25 adopted a resolution supporting Stanton's refusal. It said the resolution backed Stanton "in his efforts to establish once and for all that electronic journalism is covered by the same First Amendment guarantee enjoyed by the print media."

"The Selling of the Pentagon" continued to have many admirers. It was the recipient of one of the 1971 *Saturday Review* Television Awards "for a courageous, terse, and revealing expose of the dimensions—not generally known to the public—of the

Defense Department's use of federal tax moneys to promote and perpetuate its own bureaucratic interests, power, and privilege in the nation's military-industrial complex." The Henry W. Grady School of Journalism at the University of Georgia awarded it a special Peabody Award April 21 for "electronic journalism at its finest." The Boston University School of Public Communications honored the program April 28 with a citation saying that "the documentary, reflecting the highest standards of investigative journalism, has become a symbol of the determination of the news media to exercise and preserve their rights and responsibilities under the First Amendment, free of government interference."

CBS News President Salant, accepting the Boston honor, warned that "three decades of increasing intrusion into the delicate areas of news editing, news treatment and news judgment, no matter how nobly proposed or intended, have brought us today to a point of no return where the issue is nothing less than whether free broadcast journalism can exist." "and if free broadcast journalism cannot exist," he continued, "how secure can print journalism be? . . . For journalism, like a nation, cannot exist half free and half slave. Unless the issues which now confront us are resolved in favor of freedom, honest, independent, credible journalism . . . honest journalism is at an end."

Shortly thereafter the National Academy of Television Arts & Sciences voted to give "The Selling of the Pentagon" an Emmy Award for outstanding achievement in news documentary programming.

Senator Fulbright, noting the honors won by the CBS documentary, told the Senate May 17 that "in all the tumult, . . . no one was able to deny the basic accuracy of this program on the Pentagon's extensive public relations operations." Among additional, if minor, causes for controversy about the program were the reports that Fulbright appeared to be both the inspiration and the major source of the arguments made in "The Selling of the Pentagon." Jimmie N. Rogers and Theodore Clevenger, Jr. asserted in the October 1971 issue of the *Quarterly Journal of Speech* that in his December 1969 Senate speeches and in his book *The Pentagon Propaganda Machine,* "Fulbright had . . . laid out virtually the entire CBS case." The two writers expressed the view that the public had a right to know of the program's close following—almost point by point—of Fulbright's views and material. The documentary and its makers, however, did not mention Fulbright. At one point, Roger Mudd, as narrator, said that in preparing the program, "we sought . . . no politicians pleading special causes."

1972 Election Campaign Truce

During the early days of the 1972 election campaign, it was reported, President Nixon had issued orders to Republican campaigners to call a truce in the Administration's hostilities against the media.

An indication of this truce was said to be a speech by Agnew at a dinner of the National Newspaper Association in Portland, Ore. July 22. Agnew said in his prepared text that "the substance of my remarks is that we all, whether government official or editor, might do well to forgo harrangue and cliché in favor of discussion based on reason and public interest." He urged that "by-gone conflicts between state and press" be put aside. Agnew flew the same day to Anchorage, Alaska, where he was questioned about the Newspaper Guild's endorsement of the Democratic Presidential ticket of Senators George McGovern and Thomas F. Eagleton. Agnew described such an action by the Guild as "unusual" and expressed "hope that perhaps it will be reconsidered because it doesn't seem to be in the tradition of a separation of private opinions on behalf of the press from their function of reporting the news."

Patrick J. Buchanan, a Nixon speech-writer often credited with writing some of Agnew's more stinging attacks, was quoted in *The New York Times* August 10 as saying the truce with the media "doesn't mean that some of us have abandoned or will abandon some of our cherished assumptions about the press. But it does mean that there is little disposition around here to make an issue of the media in the campaign." *Times* correspondent Robert B. Semple, Jr. added that "nobody is authority at the White House suggests that the new approach reflects anything more than a tactical judgment" that muting criticism of the media "would be wise and useful" at the onset of a political campaign.

Senators Probe Government-Media Hostility

Senator Samuel J. Ervin (Democrat of North Carolina) and his Senate Constitutional Rights Subcommittee held several hearings in September and October 1971 and in February 1972 to investigate the role of the government in freedom of the media. Media representatives, Congress members, scholars and government officials debated charges of federal interference with press freedoms, and a variety of legislative and regulatory changes were recommended.

In announcing the hearings, Ervin had warned of "the growing deterioration of the relationship between the press and the government" and "the increasing amount of government control and influence" over broadcast news. He cited the Justice Department's June 1971 suit to prevent publication of the Pentagon Papers, a House subcommittee subpoena of materials for the CBS documentary "The Selling of the Pentagon," a Federal Communications Commission warning against broadcasting drug-related songs, and "increased use" of subpoenas to require newsmen to reveal confidential information.

Opening the hearings September 28, 1971, Ervin called it "apparent that in today's America, many people doubt the vitality and significance of the First Amendment's guarantee of freedom of the press." He cited four examples of the type of development that produced these doubts: "First, the increased subpoenaing of journalists by grand juries and Congressional committees; second, the recent publication by several newspapers of classified government information and the government's unsuccessful attempt to enjoin the publication; third, the widespread use of false press credentials by government investigators, and fourth, new fears about government control and regulation of the broadcast media."

"In addition," Ervin said," we have heard sharp and angry attacks upon the news media by high government officials. These attacks have brought fourth equally hostile responses from spokesmen for the press. Some government officials appear to believe that the purpose of the press is to present the government's policies and programs to the public in the best possible light. . . . Likewise, some members of the press appear to have forgotten that the First Amendment's guarantee of free speech and free press was not intended as their exclusive possession. Those enlightened men who devised our constitutional system did not mean to secure freedom of the press by suppressing the right of Americans, whether private citizens or public officials, to criticize the press. Not every critical word about the press is an attack on the First Amendment.

"These continuing controversies, and the bitterness and suspicion that accompany them, make it evident that many Americans are uncertain about both the role of a free press in a free society and the necessary conditions for its preservation...."

"Our historic commitment to freedom of the press means that we must tolerate absurd, misleading and vindictive reports which sometimes appear in newspapers, magazines and on radio and television," Ervin continued. "It means that thoughts and ideas which we hate and despise will appear in print and be broadcast across the land. James Madison recognized that some degree of abuse is inseparable from the proper use of everything, and in no instance is this more true than in that of the press. Most Americans have come to understand that the irritating excesses of the press are a small price to pay for a press independent of government control.

"They realize that only an independent press can vigorously and effectively contribute to that wide-ranging and critical discussion of public affairs which is a prerequisite to a democratic society. This view of the role of a free press in a free society necessarily means that there will be tension and sometimes hostility between the press and government. Indeed, it is the conflict between the press and government which attests to the vitality of the First Amendment...."

Testifying at the hearings, several media executives and newsmen complained of government intimidation. *New York Times* Executive Vice President Harding Bancroft said September 28 that the Pentagon Papers incident, in which his publication and the *Washington Post* had been enjoined from publishing secret Defense Department material for fifteen days, had set "an extremely unfortunate precedent" that might well result in "journalistic timidity or unwarranted self-censorship."

CBS President Frank Stanton October 29 and CBS newsman Walter Cronkite October 30 called for reduced government regulation of the broadcast industry. Stanton said that "over-regulation" by the FCC, especially in its application of the fairness (or equal time) doctrine, was "beginning to impede the free flow of news." Cronkite urged ending government licensing of broadcasting stations.

Several witnesses, including FCC members Dean Burch and Nicholas Johnson and NBC newscaster David Brinkley, denied that news freedom had been curtailed. Burch, a Nixon appointee, and Johnson, a liberal Democrat, maintained October 20 that the FCC had always avoided judgments about the content of news programs. Johnson said the commission had never tried "to discipline the networks in any way in response to charges of distortion." Brinkley October 19 had denied that criticism by government had hampered him in reporting the news.

Criticism of the media as insufficiently free or diverse was expressed by some witnesses, who called for stronger government supervision. Fred Friendly, former CBS news executive and currently a broadcast news professor at Columbia University, charged October 12 that the networks' profit orientation had acted to impede free and adequate news coverage and encouraged "the selling of violence and superfluous medicine." Professor Jerome A. Barron of George Washington University September 30 had proposed legislation to require the media to accept paid controversial advertising since "freedom of speech and the press is not the sole possession of those wealthy enough to own a station or a newspaper."

Legislative proposals to prevent government bodies from forcing newsmen to provide information were supported at the hearings September 28 by Senator James B. Pearson (Republican of Kansas) and Representative Charles W. Whalen (Republican of Ohio).

Ervin February 1, 1972 announced plans to seek legislation to bar Federal Bureau of Investigation probes of an individual except in criminal cases. He made this announcement at a subcommittee hearing at which CBS newsman Daniel Schorr testified on his own investigation by the FBI. The Administration had said that the White House ordered investigation of Schorr, conducted largely in August 1971, had been made to determine Schorr's fitness for a federal job for which he was being considered. Schorr testified, however, that he was first contacted by FBI agents one day after being called to the White House to hear criticism of one of his television reports. The FBI investigation was described by newsmen as an obvious case of attempted intimidation.

A year after his free-press hearings, Senator Ervin expressed his thoughts on the subject in an address delivered February 16, 1973 before a group of students and media representatives at Texas Tech University in Lubbock, Tex. "Rarely does government flagrantly violate the First Amendment," he said. "No newspapers are confiscated. No books are burned. Congress has passed no law forbidding criticism of its members. What we do have is subtle erosion—a weathering away. The pillar of press freedom is not being attacked with the picks and shovels of official censorship but by the wind and rain of threats and intimidation. The process is often almost imperceptible. The Nixon Administration has lately been charged with responsibility for a deliberate effort at erosion of press freedom. *Newsweek* magazine described the recent clashes between the media and the Administration as 'without precedent in the history of the United States.' Bill Monroe of the 'Today Show' stated that in his opinion, the Administration is trying to 'maximize governmental pressure and minimize media independence.' . . . Bill Small, CBS News Bureau chief in Washington, contends, 'There's never been a frontal assault on the press as we have now.' "

Ervin cited incidents that lent weight to charges of Nixon Administration pressure on the media: White House adviser Charles Colson predicted that the television networks "are going to be broken up one way or another . . ." because of "new technology. . . ." White House communications chief Herbert Klein telephoned NBC to complain that NBC reporter Catherine Mackin had been "unfair" to President Nixon. Presidential aide Patrick Buchanan warned that if prejudiced reporting continued, "you're going to find something done in the areas of antitrust-type action." "In 1971 we saw the White House direct the FBI to investigate CBS newsman Daniel Schorr, an Administration critic, supposedly . . . for a position of employment. . . . It was a transparent attempt at intimidation . . . by implication at all the critical reporters." The *Washington Post,* a critic of the Administration on Vietnam, was "excluded from covering the White House social events." Dr. Clay Whitehead, director of the White House Office of Telecommunications Policy, "announced an Administration proposal to condition the renewal of broadcast licenses of television stations on whether, in the judgment of the FCC, the local station management is 'substantially attuned to the needs and interests of the communities' " it serves. Whitehead later cited network news as the target and said: "Station managers and network officials who fail to act to correct imbalance or consistent bias from the networks—or who acquiesce by silence—can only be considered willing participants, to be held fully accountable . . . at license-renewal time."

Agnew on 'The Press & the Presidency'

Agnew began an address to the Minnesota Newspaper Association in Minneapolis February 23, 1973 with the assertion that "Washington reporters, with their accurate sense of contemporaneity, always believe that each new administration is plotting an assault on the freedom of the press with a determination and malignity never before seen in the Republic; the iniquities of past Presidents fade quickly in retrospect.

The words quoted, however, were not written by Agnew. They were excerpted from *A Thousand Days*, a 1965 book by Arthur Schlesinger, Jr., a member of the Kennedy Administration and critic of the Nixon Administration. Washington reporters "seemed to feel," Schlesinger wrote, "that, if a government official dared disagree with a news story, it was an attempt to 'manage' news." Schlesinger described Kennedy Administration reaction to a *Look* article about "the indignities which newspapermen were suffering under the [Kennedy] reign of terror": President John F. Kennedy "laughed and remarked, 'This is the best example of paranoia I have seen from those fellows yet.' "

Agnew, whose address was captioned "The Press and the Presidency," told the newsmen in attendance that Schlesinger's "firsthand view of relations between the Kennedy Administration and the press ten years ago deserves the attention of this audience and all those truly interested in maintaining a free and responsible American Fourth Estate. . . . My remarks . . . are directed at bringing some perspective to the questions uppermost in the minds of this audience and the American Fourth Estate generally. These questions are:

"Is there, to borrow Schlesinger's phrase, a 'reign of terror' against the press now going on in Washington?

"In the cliche-ology of the 1970s, are the Nixon Administration's press policies producing a 'chilling' effect on the First Amendment rights?

"Is the people's right to know in jeopardy today because this Administration is 'plotting an assault on the freedom of the press with a determination and malignity never before seen in the Republic'?"

Agnew replied that "the answer to those questions . . . is an emphatic 'No.' Certainly, like national administrations throughout our history, the Nixon Administration has had and will no doubt continue to have its differences with the press. That adversary relationship, as we know, is not only traditional but healthy. A pliant press is not carrying out its responsibility as an independent guardian of the public interest. Neither is a government that is pliant to the pressures of day-to-day headlines or editorial criticism necessarily carrying out its long-range responsibilities to the enational interest...."

"When editorial and Administration opinions differ," Agnew asked, "why cannot the differences be accepted as sincere judgments by both sides? ... Why cannot a public official criticize the editorial advocates for emphasizing that which supports their opinions and playing down that which contradicts them? After all, editors are only human. They are subject to the same business pressures, need for peer approval and pride in the efficacy of their opinions that affect the rest of us fallible mortals.

"Yet some prestigious media spokesmen can be read and heard almost daily expressing fear for the future of the First Amendment. They assert that the American people are being kept in the dark by a repressive government. A national network newsman has referred to an Administration 'conspiracy' against the people's right to know.

"It is hard to find any factual basis for this hysteria. Almost nothing goes on in government that is not examined, re-examined, plumbed, analyzed, guessed about, criticized and caricatured in the media.... Under our system, the exceptional good judgment of the American people ... represents the first line of defense against potential assault on the First Amendment or any other of our precious Constitutional freedoms. Resort to hyperbole and the indiscriminate application of terms such as 'repression' and 'conspiracy' only undermine the credibility of such critics with a general public which, as Schlesinger noted, has heard it all before...."

Agnew said that a recent Alfred Dupont-Columbia University Survey of Broadcast Journalism had indicated "a loss of credibility by television network news among the viewing public." "Predictably," he said, "those who conducted the survey try to trace this development to Administration criticism of the media." Agnew suggested, however, that "in the television news industry's response to these results a degree of self-analysis rather than a search for outside scapegoats would seem to be in order." He held that "if media representatives wish to invoke a privilege unique to their profession, the profession itself must promulgate and enforce standards for the protection of the general community. Otherwise, individuals will have no defense against character assaults through the willful or negligent use of unidentified sources. ..."

Agnew asserted that "the Nixon Administration is no more desirous of nor more capable of curtailing freedom of the press in America than any of its predecessors. On the contrary, . . . news coverage of government today is more intensive than ever before in American history."

"However," Agnew warned, "an increase in intensity of coverage does not necessarily mean an increase in information. The new 'advocacy journalism' often foreswears objectivity in the interest of what the reporter perceives to be a high moral purpose. The effect of a reporter's zealous dedication to a cause results in a focus of heat more often than light. The antidote . . . is not more thousands of words supportive of a reporter's personal conclusions, but diversity of opinion. Such diversity provides the best protection against the danger of censorship. ..."

Agnew denied that the "fundamental issue"—the "major areas of contention between government and the press today"—truly involved "incursions of government power into press rights and prerogatives." The real involvement, he held, was "the point at which the rights and prerogatives of a free press interface those of other institutions and rights in a free society." These questions, he said, concerned not only First Amendment interests of the press but "rights and interests accorded . . . all Americans under the other parts of the Constitution" and "the fundamental interest of society in the proper administration of justice under a system providing due process."

"A speech by a government official discussing these problems does not constitute a threat to First Amendment rights," Agnew declared. "Nor do two speeches . . . constitute a conspiracy. Indeed, the discourse between government and Fourth Estate in resolving such problems must necessarily be a dialogue, not a monologue. And a dialogue entitles a government official, as much as a network newsman, to tell the American people the way *he* thinks it is on any given day."

Agnew said that "the most extreme example of . . . oversimplification of rights and responsibilities . . . is to be found in the contention of some adherents of a so-called 'New Journalism' that they are answerable to a supra-institutional code, independent of the free society in which they operate." Rejecting such views, Agnew asserted that no institution—government or press—had "a monopoly on truth or on the zeal to pursue truth in the public interest."

CBS Drops 'Instant Analysis,' then Resumes It

More than two and a half years after Agnew (in November 1969) attacked television networks for broadcasting "instant analysis and querulous criticism" of Presidential speeches immediately after the addresses were delivered, CBS announced June 6, 1973 that it was discontinuing the practice. CBS Chairman William S. Paley reported that commentary on Presidential speeches would be carried on normal news programs. After a speech about which there might be "significant national disagreement," CBS said, its network would give free time, usually within a week, to the holders of opposing views. Spokesmen for NBC and ABC said their networks were not changing their policies on such commentary.

The new CBS policy lasted only five months. The company then announced November 12 that it was ending its ban on instant analysis of Presidential statements. Paley said that while the additional time for reflection and research might enhance the network's coverage, the "rapid series of exceptionally newsworthy events" had made it clear that postponing news analysis under all circumstances may impair a journalistic service of far greater value to the public than we had realized." He added that the network would continue its policy of giving free time to qualified spokesmen for opposing views.

Views Differ on Administration's Attacks

The struggle between the networks and the Nixon Administration seemed to be under constant evaluation by people on both sides of the issue.

Four television anchormen met with *New York Times* editors and discussed the matter in March 1973. The TV representatives were John Chancellor, Walter Cronkite, Harry Reasoner and Howard K. Smith, and their answere to *Times* questions were published in the *Times* March 12. According to all four, the

Administration campaign had produced little or no ill effects on network performance. But Cronkite, with at least Chancellor's support, suggested that the Administration was deliberately undermining press freedoms.

The anchormen were asked, "Starting with Vice President Agnew, have the attacks by the Administration affected TV coverage in any way?"

Chancellor said he "saw a certain drawing back, I think, in being more careful on the part of journalism in America generally. . . . I think people in our business, before they use a certain word or phrase, ought to think twice about it. And I think for a period there people were thinking three times. I don't personally, in my own work and in the network's work, see that there have been any serious changes of any kind." He added later that "we [journalists] may all be doing our jobs better because the Administration has accused us of being biased against them."

Smith said the Administration attack "has no effect whatever. If it does make people think three times instead of twice, I think that's good. In fact, I think five times before I say something." He had asserted earlier: "It seems to me that if we give them [the Administration] hell, they've got the right to give us hell."

Cronkite said that "probably these attacks have helped us pull up our boots a little bit and practice our profession with a little more expertise than we applied before, perhaps. . . . But it's a side effect from what the intent was, and I cannot agree in any way with the intent." As for whether the attacks had "affected us as to the courage with which we tackle the Administration," Cronkite said, "the clear indications are that that is not the case. And we're in trouble because of it." He suggested the possibility that Administration attacks "had a subconscious effect, and that worries me a great deal. . . ." In discussion earlier of proposed changes in television-station licensing legislation, Cronkite had said Administration proposals indicated "that there's no retreat on the part of the Administration from what I believe to be its firm intent to drag down the press and all of us in broadcast journalism as well."

Cronkite said later that "what I object to in the criticism from the White House is not the fact that there is criticism, not even the fact that they would try to raise their own credibility by attacking ours. But what has happened is that this Administration, through what I believe to be a considered and concerted campaign, has so managed to politicize the issue of the press versus the Administration that now we come to the real crunch, which is the matter of our actual freedoms to operate, our freedom to criticize, our right to do that, our ability to function as journalists without harassment by an offended grand jury. . . . We've come to that dangerous state now where the press is in a position that to defend the right of the people to know—that is, to defend freedom of speech and press—is somehow or other to be anti-Administration. . . . [The Administration has thus] created two Americas—one that believes in freedom of speech and press and one that doesn't."

Herbert G. Klein, the Nixon White House's director of communications, chose a group of journalists—the National Press Club in Washington—for a March 26, 1973 address denying media charges that the Nixon Administration was an active enemy of freedom of the press.

Klein held that the charges "are much exaggerated, such as Dean Sayre's comment that this is the time of the most insidious threat to the press since Joe McCarthy," or Benjamin Bradlee's remark "to the effect that the First Amendment is under the greatest threat in our time." "I believe," Klein said, "that, on some occasions, the press becomes oversensitive and perhaps over-alarmist in where we really are in terms of the relationship between government and press and how free the press really is. I submit that the press is not intimidated, should not be, never will be. . . ." "While I believe that the best protection for the press is for the press to fight for its rights," Klein said, he held that "a statement that the press is about to lose in all parts of the free enterprise system and that the press and the First Amendment are in grave danger is over-exaggerated. . . ."

The Professional Relations Committee of the National Press Club June 12, 1973 approved a statement concluding "that the Nixon Administration has engaged in an unprecedented, governmentwide effort to control, restrict and conceal information to which the public is entitled, and has conducted for its own political purposes a concerted campaign to discredit the press." It held that the Nixon Administration then appeared "unwilling to accept the traditional role of an independent press in a free society."

These conclusions were made public as part of an analysis of the Nixon Administration's relations with the media. The study was made for the National Press Club by the Department of Communications of American University in Washington, D.C. Professor Lewis W. Wolfson headed the study.

In interviews conducted between November 1972 and March 1973 with members of the Washington press corps and with the "only three out of the fifteen White House officials we approached [who] would join in the spirit of the study," the questioners said, they had "found in the press corps an overwhelming feeling that Washington's traditional adversary jousting between journalists and officials had deepened into an attempted freeze by government on any but the most superficial 'straight news' reporting of the Nixon presidency."

According to the study, "even in the worst moments in previous administrations, correspondents felt, most Washington-wise politicians seemed to adopt certain unwritten rules for their encounters with news people. The adversary battle was a love-hate relationship. You talked to the press, even if you wanted to say as little as possible. You were friendly when it served your purposes, suddenly unavailable when you didn't want to talk. . . . You gave a little to get a little, and everybody had a vague feeling that somehow good government was being served, even if journalists and politicians could never agree on exactly what the public should know" about events in Washington.

The Nixon Administration, the correspondents said, was "not inclined to abide by the traditional adversary conventions. From there it was only a small step to trying to put the press on the defensive by discrediting its reports about government." Nixon Administration officials were accused of "framing a policy of massive official hostility to all but a few, selected portions of the news media—even while they argued that it was the press that was overreacting to *their* criticism."

Alan Otten, Washington bureau chief of the *Wall Street Journal*, was quoted as saying the Nixon Administration was "probably the most closed administration since I've been in Washington, and that goes over twenty-five years." Otten held that the purpose of much of Vice President Agnew's attacks on the media "was not to set the record straight but to intimidate the press—particularly television and radio, which are more directly subject to government control. . . . [T]hey have succeeded to a considerable degree in intimidating some people, particularly in the broadcasting field, and making other people lean over backwards to give them a much fairer shake than they sometimes deserve." Otten asserted that the Nixon Administration's key people did not understand the traditional relationship between officials and journalists "and just completely regard us as the enemy."

CBS correpondent Dan Rather expressed a belief "that there are certain people within this administration who sincerely believe that theirs has been an open administration" while others "know damned well that it hasn't been." In "the most important way—the accessability to the President himself—this administration has been closed," he declared. Rather said that Agnew "latched onto popular . . . suspicions about journalism and a few truths. . . . And whether he intended to do so or not, he used the traditional technique of the demagogue in pitting one group of people against another. . . . [T]his has had an adverse effect because it has poisoned the air. It has [caused] unnecessary rancor between reporters and their sources, and between reporters and the public. . . ."

Garnett Horner, White House correspondent for the *Washington Star-News*, was quoted as saying he thought the openness of the Nixon Administration was "on a par. . . . I think we get more information than ever . . . in this administration that in some previous ones. . . . If a reporter has a reputation for being fair and honest and not out to advocate an adverse point of view—not out to make a monkey out of somebody—he can generally get to see whomever he wants to." Raymond McHugh, bureau chief of Copley News Service, said he had seen three administrations "and would rate them just about even" on openness. The snydicated columnist Robert Novak said that the Nixon Administration was the fourth he had covered, and none of them has been very open."

Clark R. Mollenhoff, bureau chief of the *Des Moines Register and Tribune* and former special counsel to Nixon, was quoted as saying that in withholding information, the Nixon Administration had a "tendency—as every administration has—to fail to distinguish between their own political security and national security." He said Agnew's criticisms of the media "probably were ill-advised, but they were accurate on facts. . . . He's got every right to . . . argue with the press on anything. We certainly should not be above criticism. The problem [comes] when they suggest governmental control or cutting into our free access" to information. Agnew's criticisms, Mollenhoff said, "are a hell of a lot less of a menace than is the negligence of the press itself in not taking care of its own rights."

Max Frankel, Sunday editor of *The New York Times,* told the interviewers that he did not regard Agnew's comments "as serious or meaningful journalistic criticism." According to Frankel, Agnew "was engaged in a political exercise against certain parts of the press. The fact is that he has not been exercised at all about some of the worst performers in the press field . . . because their political communes are closer to his. . . . I think it is a mockery that he . . . [picked] on the most effective journalistic operations."

Peter Lisagor, bureau chief of the *Chicago Daily News,* said that in many cases, Agnew's attacks on the media "created kind of a psychological undertow that forced some people in our business to pull their punches, to be a little more cautious than they might be justified in being." As for the media-government adversary relationship, Lisagor said that Administration officials "would like to make cheerleaders out of newsmen. And when newsmen don't agree to be cheerleaders, we have the constant struggle to find out more than they want us to know. . . . And as long as we represent the public's interest, we'd better keep at it as aggressively as we can. I suspect that the more aggressive we are, the less inclined they may be to withhold" information. Lisagor agreed that "most reporters do tend to be liberal" but denied that this affected their writing. "I know some of the most prejudiced people in this town who are straight, honest, objective reporters. . . . I know people who hate given government officials, and write very straight accounts about them." The charges of liberal bias, he said, "simply ignore the fact that there is a high degree of professionalism in the press corps."

Benjamin Bradlee, executive editor of the *Washington Post,* suggested that Agnew's critiques "probably had a good effect overall because they've made the intelligent editor be self-critical and examine the [journalistic] decision-making processes. . . . But it also has had a negative effect in making it popular to be critical of one of the major institutions of a democratic society. I don't think a society whose institutions are constantly under attack and disbelieved is healthy. . . ."

White House director of communications Herbert G. Klein was one of the three Administration officials who agreed to be interviewed. He also was one of the few praised by the newsmen interviewed as trying to open channels of communication between the media and the administration. Klein denied that Agnew's criticisms of the media were intimidating. "I guess that I've answered more questions from newsmen . . . than anybody in the Administration," he said, "and in four years I've not met an intimidated reporter. . . . I think the idea of intimidation by the Administration is not well-taken at all. . . ."

DeVan Shumway, public affairs director of the Committee for the Re-election of the President, another Nixon official who agreed to be interviewed, denied that the Administration had encroached on some news freedoms. "I think the press is a little oversensitive to criticism of itself," he said ". . . There's a sensitivity in the press that when you criticize them and you're in an official government position, you're stepping" on freedom-of-the-press rights. "Well, your're not," Shumway declared. ". . . You're protecting that right."

White House Memos Reveal Anti-Media Planning

In 1973 it became clear that President Nixon had instructed aides to counter media criticism as early as 1969 and that action against detractors in the media was being planned at that time. This was revealed in a series of White House memoranda made public October 31 and November 1, 1973 by Republican Senator Lowell P. Weicker, Jr. of Connecticut. The memos, by various White House aides but not by Nixon himself, discussed ways of applying pressure to make sure that the media were "fair" to the Nixon Administration. Suggested methods of persuasion included "the possible threat of anti-trust action" and "a threat of IRS [tax] investigation."

The earliest of the White House papers, dated October 17, 1969, was a memo by Jeb S. Magruder, a Presidential aide, to H. R. Haldeman, Nixon's chief of staff. In the message, Magruder noted that "yesterday you [Haldeman] asked me to give you a talking paper on specific problems we've had in shot-gunning the media and anti-Administration spokesmen on unfair coverage." It said Magruder was enclosing "aprproximately twenty-one requests from the President in the last thirty days requesting specific action relating to what could be considered unfair news coverage. . . . I would gather that there have been at least double or triple that many requests . . . to accomplish the same objective."

"The real problem," Magruder wrote, ". . . is to get this unfair coverage in such a way that we make major impact on a basis which the networks-newspapers and Congress will react to and begin to look at things somewhat differently." Among Magruder's proposals:

"1. Begin an official monitoring system through the FCC as soon as Dean Burch is officially on board as chairman. If the monitoring system proves our point, we have then legitimate and legal rights to go to the networks, etc., and make official complaints from the FCC. This will have much more effect than a phone call from Herb Klein or Pat Buchanan.

"2. Utilize the anti-trust devision [of the Department of Justice] to investigate various media relating to antitrust violations. Even the possible threat of anti-trust action I think would be effective in changing their views in the above matter.

"3. Utilizing the Internal Revenue Service as a method to look into the various organizations that we are most concerned about. Just a threat of an IRS investigation will probably turn their approach.

"4. Begin to show favorites within the media. Since they are basically not on our side let us pick the favorable ones as Kennedy did. . . . [B]y being open we have not gotten anyone to back us on a consistent basis and many of those who were favorable toward us are now giving it to us at various times, i.e. Ted Lewis, Hugh Sidey. . . ."

Critics of the Administration had charged long before Weicker turned up the Magruder memo that actions of the sort Magruder had suggested were being taken by the Administration in what were deemed to be efforts to intimidate the media.

The twenty-one Presidential requests for action on allegedly unfair media coverage appeared to be largely requests for reports on specific items or instructions to Administration personnel to present the Nixon viewpoint to the public or to the news people whose reports were considered unfair. Examples were: (a) a September 20 request of the President to communications director Herbert Klein "that you inform [columnist] Walter Trohan about our substantive programs and that you place the blame for inaction on the Democratic Congerss"; (b) a September 23 request to Presidential aide John Ehrlichman "for a report on possible answers to Evans-Novak charge of an Administration retreat on tax reform"; (c) a September 26 request to Herbert Klein "that you contact Howard K. Smith and give him the true record on what the Administration has done"; (d) a September 30 request to Klein "for letters to the editor regarding *Newsweek's* lead article covering the President's U.N. speech"; (e) an October 3 request to Klein "that we have the *Chicago Tribune* hit Senator Percy hard on his ties with the peace group." Some of the Presidential requests seemed to relate exclusively to relations with political figures. The requests appeared to make no suggestions similar to Magruder's proposals.

In a confidential memo to Magruder March 9, 1970, Haldeman said he had "talked with Connie Stuart about the need to follow up on the highly inaccurate article in the *New York Times Magazine* . . . regarding White House social activities. There are numerous factual errors and other very erroneous implications. I suggested to Connie that she might want to give the facts to another rival columnist and let him go to town and start a battle. . . . They should not be allowed to get away with this. . . . Would you please give me once every two weeks a summary of the various hatchet-man operations—letters to the editors, counterattack, etc., so that I can report to the President on the activity in this regard. . . ."

In a "secret" memo July 16, 1970, Lawrence Higby, Haldeman's aide, told Magruder that "as I indicated to you . . ., we need to get some creative thinking going on an attack on [TV newscaster Chet] Huntley for his [anti-Nixon] statements in *Life*. One thought that comes to mind is getting all the people to sign a petition calling for the immediate removal of Huntley right now. . . . What we are trying to do here is to tear down the institution. Huntley will go out in a blaze of glory and we should attempt to pop his bubble. . . . [T]here are many . . . things that we can do such as getting independent station owners to write NBC saying that they should remove Huntley now. . . ."

Magruder next day sent Haldeman and Klein a "confidential/eyes only" memo outlining "a tentative plan on press objectivity." The memo said that Huntley (identified only as a prominent television newscaster) "intends to send a letter to the editor of the magazine claiming he was misquoted and will also send a letter of apology to the President." The Magruder plan's objective, Magruder wrote, was "to question the overall objectivity of a television newscaster who has expressed opinionated views in an influential consumer publication while still employed as a supposedly objective television newscaster. . . ." Magruder proposed to extend the questioning of Huntley's actions and motives to "the professional objectivity and ethics of the whole media and to generate a public re-examination of the role of the media in American life."

Magruder's memo listed eighteen specific proposals from various Nixon Administration officials as part of the overall plan. The proposals included: (a) a plan by Herbert Klein to "plant a column with a syndicated columnist which raises the question of objectivity and ethics in the news media"; (b) Patrick Buchanan's proposal to "ask the Vice President to speak out on this issue" and possibly "point out that the *Life* quote has proved his point"; (c) Franklin C. Nofziger's suggestion that "Dean Burch 'express concern' about press objectivity in response to a letter from a Congressman"; (d) Charles W. Colson's plan to "have outside groups petition the FCC and issue public 'statements of concern' over press objectivity"; (e) Magruder's proposal to "form a blue-ribbon media 'watchdog' committe to report to the public on cases of biased reporting"; (f) Nofziger's proposal to "have a Senator or Congressman write a public letter to the FCC suggesting the 'licensing' of individual newsmen"; (g) Klein's plan, "through contacts in the ASNE and NAB, [to] bring up the question of a 'fairness pledge' for members."

In an "administratively confidential" memo to Higby August 28, 1970, Magruder said that the Huntley issue "is fairly well played out. We leaked his letter of apology . . . and it got very good coverage. We will continue to hammer at press favoritism on a regular basis. We will ask the Vice President to make this a standard fare while he is on the stump in the Congressional campaign. . . . [T]he general question can be kept in the news as we find more and more examples of unfair treatment by the press. This will simply be a continuing function."

A direct confrontation between White House aide Charles Colson and what appeared to be a timorous group of television officials—"the three network chief executives"—was described by Colson in a memo to Herbert Klein and H. R. Haldeman dated September 25, 1970. Colson made it plain that he thought media fear of the Administration's regulative power should be used as a weapon to achieve Nixon goals. The "FYI—Eyes only, please" message summarized the confrontation thus:

"1. The networks are terribly nervous over the uncertain state of the law, i.e., the recent FCC decisions and the pressure to grant

Congress access to TV. They are also apprehensive about us. . . . The harder I pressed them (CBS and NBC), the more accommodating, cordial and almost apologetic they became. [CBS President Frank Stanton for all this bluster is the most insecure of all.

"2. There was unanimous agreement that the President's right of access to TV should in no way be restrained. Both CBS and ABC agreed with me that on most occasions the President speaks as President and that there is no obligation for presenting a contrasting point of view under the Fairness Doctrine (This, by the way, is not the law—the FCC has always ruled that the Fairness Doctrine always applies—and either they don't know that or they are willing to concede us the point.) NBC . . . argues that the fairness test must be applied to every Presidential speech but [NBC President Julian] Goodman is also quick to agree that there are probably instances in which Presidential addresses are not 'controversial' under the Fairness Doctrine and, therefore, there is no duty to balance. All agree no one has a right of 'reply' and that fairness doesn't mean answering the President but rather is 'issue oriented.' . . . What is important is that they know how strongly we feel about this.

"4. They are terribly concerned with being able to work out their own policies with respect to balanced coverage and not to have policies imposed on them by either the Commission [FCC] or the Congress. ABC and CBS said that they felt we could, however, through the FCC make any policies we wanted to. (This is worrying them all.)

"5. To my surprise, CBS did not deny that the news had been slanted against us. [CBS Chairman William S.] Paley merely said that every Administration has felt the same way and that we have been slower in coming to them to complain than our predecessors. He, however, ordered Stanton in my presence to review the analysis with me and if the news has not been balanced to see that the situation is immediately corrected. . . .

"6. CBS does not defend the O'Brien appearance. [Democratic National Chairman Lawrence F. O'Brien had been given CBS air time to answer President Nixon's policy statements. A Republican complaint accused O'Brien of making "partisan" use of the privilege.] Paley wanted to make it very clear that it would not happen again and that they would not permit partisan attacks on the President. . . .

The Media Versus the Nixon Administration

"7. ABC and NBC believe that the whole controversy over 'answers' to the President can be handled by giving some time regularly to presentations by the Congress. . . . In this regard, ABC will do anything we want. NBC proposes to provide a very limited Congressional coverage once or twice a year and additionally once a year 'loyal opposition' type answers to the President's State of the Union address (which has been the practice since 1966). CBS takes quite a different position. Paley's policy is that the Congress cannot be the sole balancing mechanism and that the Democratic leadership in Congress should have time to present Democratic viewpoints on legislation. (On this point, which may become the most critical of all, we can split the networks in a way that will be very much to our advantage.)"

Colson reported that "the networks badly went to have these kinds of discussions which they said they had with other Administrations but never with ours. They told me anytime we had a complaint about slanted coverage for me to call them directly. Paley said that he would like to come down to Washington to spend time with me anytime that I wanted. In short, they are very much afraid of us and are trying hard to prove they are 'good guys.'

"These meetings had a very salutary effect in letting them know that we are determined to protect the President's position, that we know precisely what is going on from the standpoint of both law and policy and that we are not going to permit them to get away with anything that interferes with the President's ability to communicate. Paley made the point that he was amazed at how many people agree with the Vice President's criticism of the networks. He also went out of his way to say how much he supports the President. . . . [T]hey are damned nervous and scared and we should continue to take a very tough line, face to face, and in other ways. . . ."

Colson proposed continuing the pressure on the networks. Among his plans, he said he would "pursue with Dean Burch the possibility of . . . [a favorable] ruling by the FCC on the role of the President when he uses TV. . . . [This] would, of course, have an inhibiting impact on the networks and their professed concern with achieving balance." Colson said he was "realistic enough to realize that we probably won't see any obvious improvement in the news coverage but I think we can dampen their ardor for putting on 'loyal opposition' type programs."

Attempt to Control Public Broadcasting

Attempts by the Nixon Administration to control public broadcasting between 1969 and 1974 were revealed in 1979 through White House memoranda obtained by *The New York Times* under the Freedom of Information Act. The paper printed excerpts of the memos February 24. While no single memo described a master plan, taken together, according to the *Times*, they disclosed a scheme by the Nixon Administration to mold public broadcasting politically. The strategy included:

(1) Gaining control of the board of the Corporation for Public Broadcasting (CPB) through Presidential appointments.

(2) Making an issue of the high salaries paid to Sander Vanocur and Robert MacNeil, who were then two of public broadcasting's most respected journalists. (Vanocur earned $85,000 a year, MacNeil $65,000.)

(3) Exploiting the issue of national versus local station control in the system. The national programming entities—the Public Broadcasting Service and the National Public Affairs Center for Television (NPACT)—were considered politically liberal by the Nixon White House.

(4) Banishing national news and public affairs programs from the system by breaking up the then-emerging public broadcasting network and channeling a large share of federal funds to local stations.

(5) Cutting off federal funds to National Educational Television (NET, since merged into WNET/13 of New York City). NET, a major programming source, had received most of its financing from the Ford Foundation and was viewed by the Administration as an originator of liberal-slanted programs.

In one memo, dated June 18, 1971, Peter Flanigan, a White House assistant, wrote to President Nixon that there were "two alternatives which we may pursue with respect to CPB: either (1) attempt to kill it or (2) attempt to shape its future organization and direction." Flanigan rejected the first alternative as "politically difficult" in view of CPB's "strong educational support and generally favorable image." Of the second alternative, Flanigan said that the Nixon Administration had an "opportunity to establish, by legislation or otherwise, structures and counterbalances which will restrain [CPB's liberal] tendency in future years and which, as a political matter, it will be difficult for other administrations to alter."

A memo dated November 24, 1971 was sent to H. R. Haldeman, White House chief of staff, by Clay T. Whitehead, director of the Office of Telecommunications Policy. "After Vanocur and MacNeil were announced in late September," the Whitehouse memo read, "we planted with the trade press the idea that their obvious liberal bias would reflect adversely on public television. . . . Public television stations throughout the country were unhappy that once again they were being given programs from Washington and New York without participating in the decisions." Whitehead said that a speech he had made "criticizing the increasing centralization of public television . . . has widened the credibility gap between local stations and CPB." Whitehead detailed plans to "quietly solicit critical articles regarding Vanocur's salary coming from public funds" and to "quietly encourage station managers throughout the country to put pressure on NPACT and CPB to put balance in their programming or risk the possibility of local stations not carrying these programs."

The *Times* reported that Administration efforts to control the CPB board had failed by the time Nixon resigned in 1974. However, the newspaper claimed that four board members met frequently with White House officials and kept them apprised of the board's policies and program proposals. The four were identified as Albert L. Cole, a director of the *Reader's Digest* and Nixon's first appointee to the board; Jack Wrather, a television and film producer; Thomas W. Moore, a former president of the ABC-TV network, and Thomas B. Curtis, a former Republican Congressman from Missouri who became president of CPB with White House backing. Curtis resigned the post in 1973 after a dispute with the board and the Administration. Henry Loomis, current president of CPB, was also said to have had close ties with the Nixon Administration. The *Times* reported that Loomis had made a practice of meeting with Whitehead before every board meeting.

The Downfall of Nixon & Agnew

Spiro T. Agnew's role in the Nixon Administration's war on the media—and in the Administration itself—came to an end October 10, 1973 when Agnew resigned as Vice President to avoid prosecution on charges of bribery, conspiracy and tax evasion. Faced with an apparently airtight case against him, Agnew pleaded no contest to a tax count in satisfaction of all the charges against him.

Richard M. Nixon was brought down by the Watergate scandal. The Watergate affair began during the 1972 Presidential primary election campaign when five men broke into the headquarters of the Democratic National Committee in the Watergate office-and-hotel complex in Washington. They were arrested there by the police at 2 a.m. June 17. Their seizure led to a series of events that ultimately resulted August 9, 1974 in Nixon's resignation as President. He resigned as the House of Representatives was preparing to impeach him.

The long and often confusing Congressional and press investigations that followed the Watergate break-in produced conflicting evidence that White House and Nixon reelection officials were involved in a plot to spy on the Democratic headquarters. Several close Nixon associates were convicted and jailed for their part in the affair. Nixon insisted that he was not involved in the political espionage conspiracy or in the illegal effort to cover it up, but he did admit to wrong judgments in handling the situation. He said on resigning that he was leaving office because "America needs a full-time President and a full-time Congress." "To continue to fight through the months ahead for my personal vindication would almost totally absorb the time and attention of both the President and the Congress," he declared.

The Watergate story, intensively covered by the press, had aggravated the antagonism between the Nixon Administration and the media. *Washington Post* reporters Carl Bernstein and Bob Woodward were generally regarded as having performed the outstanding investigative reporting on the case—and as sharing much of the credit for uncovering the White House's connection with the conspiracy.

In a nationally televised broadcast April 30, 1973, Nixon had accepted responsibility for the Watergate affair, although he insisted that he was not personally involved in it. Shortly after making his speech, Nixon appeared in the White House press room, where some fifteen reporters and photographes were gathered. "Ladies and gentlemen of the press," he told them, "we have had our differences in the past, and I hope you give me hell every time you think I'm wrong. I hope I'm worthy of your trust." Then he left.

White House Press Secretary Ronald L. Ziegler was asked by a reporter May 1 whether he would apologize to the *Washington Post* for previous denunciations of its Watergate coverage. He said he would. Ziegler had accused the *Post* and its reporters of "shabby journalism" and "a blatant effort at character assassination." He said *Post* reporters Bernstein and Woodward had pursued the story vigorously and deserved the credit they were receiving. "When we're wrong, we're wrong," Ziegler conceded, "and I would have to say I was in that case and other cases." The apology was "accept[ed] . . . with pleasure" by *Post* publisher Katharine Graham later May 1. "We appreciate it," she said, noting that "the Administration was trying to undermine the credibility of the press for the last ten months."

But Agnew, then still Vice President, denounced the "techniques" used by the media in reporting on Watergate as "a very short jump from McCarthyism." Asserting that there had been "a great amount of hearsay" and use of material from unnamed sources, Agnew May 8 chided the press as "overzealous" on Watergate. "I applaud the efforts and I applaud the results," he declared, "but I cannot applaud the techniques being used." Senator William Proxmire, the Wisconsin Democrat, asserted in a Senate speech May 8 that the press was "grossly unfair" to Nixon. Nixon was being "tried, sentenced and executed by rumor and allegation," and this was analogous to "McCarthyistic destruction," Proxmire said. He praised the press, however, for a "superb job" in uncovering the Watergate facts.

At a press conference October 26, 1973, Nixon said he had "never heard or seen such outrageous, vicious, distorted reporting in twenty-seven years of public life." "I'm not blaming anybody for that" he continued. "Perhaps what happened is that what we did brought it about, and therefore the media decided that they would have to take that particular line. But when people are pounded night after night with that kind of frantic, hysterical reporting, it naturally shakes their confidence."

Deputy White House Press Secretary Gerald L. Warren lectured White House correspondents October 29 on the President's insistence on "perspective" in their reporting. He indicated his displeasure with specific television broadcasts. Nixon speechwriter Patrick Buchanan appeared on a CBS morning news program October 29. He compared the mood at the Nixon press conference to that of a bull ring and gave his "personal" recommendation that the Administration make a legislative effort "to break the power of the networks." Nixon's son-in-law, David Eisenhower, appeared on an NBC-TV interview program October 30. He said that there was too much "reporting without applying any perspective to it at all." In his view, he said, the "irresponsibility" of the media had been "matched by the irresponsibility of the people they may quote."

The New York Times reported November 5 that the White House had been compiling a list of alleged "sins" committed by the media, especially television, against Nixon. The *Times* suggested that the list had been the basis for Nixon's October 26 attack on the media. Among the items on the list was an analysis of news coverage by the three television networks October 22, the first weekday after the Administration's dismissal of special Watergate prosecutor Archibald Cox. The programs contained nineteen spots the White House considered unfavorable to Nixon, two spots considered favorable and one judged neutral, the *Times* reported. Ken W. Clawson, director of the White House Office of Communications, said: "Were those nienteen television spots reporting, or were they creating an impeachment atmosphere? That day on television was probably the last straw for the President—the outcries for impeachment on television in the wake of the Cox firing."

The pressure for impreachment—intensified by media coverage of Watergate revelations—continued to grow. Nixon finally avoided impeachment by quitting the Presidency.

Performance of the Media

Monitoring the Media

Among the frequent controversies involving the media are those that question its performance and reliability. Is the media accurate? Is it honest? Does it distort? Is it impartial? Is it fair? Does it provide full information on essential topics? Does it present all newsworthy positions on controversial issues? Does it fail to cover newsworthy events? Is it controlled by big business—or other selfish interests? These questions are not all easy to answer satisfactorily, as the case of "The Selling of the Pentagon" has demonstrated.

Lester Markel, former Sunday editor of *The New York Times*, wrote in the September 15, 1972 edition of *World* magazine that there were "solid reasons" for the widespread mistrust of many newspapers: "Inaccuracy (shoddy reporting, sensational editing, lack of perspective); irresponsibility (abandonment of objectivity, disregard for national security, disinterest in the public interest); inaccessibility (blindness to minority viewpoints, identification with the Establishment roster and dogma)." In addition, Markel cited the staging of events, incitements to violence and pandering in general.

The "worst mistake" made by the press, said Norman Isaacs, former president of the American Society of Newspaper Editors, is its failure to correct its many inaccuracies. Speaking on the

Public Broadcasting Service program "The Advocates" March 3, 1973, he reported on a study he had made. Of 112 newspapers he had checked around the country, Isaacs said, "only twelve have any formal policy of making corrections. Eighty-eight of those which do not have any policy have no intention of instituting any formal policy of making corrections. It's just paranoid."

A recurrent suggestion is that a respected body be formed to monitor the media. As proposed by some, such an organ could be composed entirely of media people and thus be a self-monitoring group. To counter the criticism that a panel made up only of media people would have a pro-media bias—or would at least be presumed to have such a leaning—others suggest that a monitoring group should include a sizable proportion of non-media people.

Some media people say that the suggestions for a monitoring group seem justified. Others reject them as threatening freedom of the press. According to many newsmen, media freedom will be best served if each newspaper and broadcast organization judges its performance by itself without interference by government or non-government monitors. A viable publication or broadcasting station should be able to improve its performance and correct its failures without coercion, many editors assert. It is pointed out that newspapers frequently do print corrections—even without a formal policy—and that an occasional publication (e.g., the *Washington Post*) has even appointed an ombudsman to call attention publicly to its flaws. A few publications devoted to criticism of the press have also appeared.

There probably is no established publication or broadcasting company that has not been involved in some way at least in some of the controversies over media performance. It would be impossible to record them all. Those that are detailed in this book, therefore, are chosen simply as representative events that illustrate the reasons for the major media controversies.

A citizens group named Accuracy in Media (AIM) was formed in Washington in 1969 to keep an eye on media correctness and fairness. It became involved in several of the media controversies of the early 1970s.

With Abraham H. Kalish, a retired professor of communications, as its executive secretary, AIM studied, tabulated and rated media coverage of a variety of major events and sought to bring its findings to the attention of the media, the public and, especially, the publications or broadcasting systems whose performance it found inaccurate, unfair or otherwise wanting.

Reporting on AIM less than two years after the organization appeared, *Editor & Publisher*'s August 21, 1971 issue noted such AIM achievements as: "a detailed critique of CBS documentaries, 'The Selling of the Pentagon,' and 'Sixty Minutes' on Castro's Cuba"; "a detailed report on . . . coverage of the House Internal Security Committee hearings on the antiwar protests in Washington last spring"; a report on "seriously misleading" editing of the NBC documentary "Say Goodbye"; *National Review*'s agreement, on AIM's demand, that it correct "an erroneous quote attributed to Representative William R. Anderson of Tennessee."

But "Kalish acknowledges that many of AIM's protests and citations of errors have either drawn irritated responses or been ignored," *Editor & Publisher* said. Kalish was cited as holding that AIM has no interest in any medium's ideology. According to *Editor & Publisher*, Kalish said that AIM's objective was "that the media report news that the public is entitled to know, and not supress, ignore, or distort news" because of disagreement "with the content or the angle of the story."

Kalish was described as "something of a burr under the saddle of editors . . . who consider it their prerogative to acknowledge, and in some cases correct, their own mistakes. . . ." News executives have made it clear that many editors would similarly object to anybody else who called attention to their prejudices and errors.

The establishment of a "center for media study" that would judge the performance of the press and broadcasters had also been recommended in a task force report released without comment January 12, 1970 by the National Commission on the Causes & Prevention of Violence. In its 614-page report—"Mass Media and Violence"—the task force said the news media could reduce the potential for violence in America by "functioning as a faithful conduit for intergroup communication, providing a true market place of ideas . . . and reducing the incentive to confrontation that sometimes erupts in violence." The independent council on mass media was one of the panel's recommendations to make the media more responsive to the public.

The task force proposed that the center study the performance of the news media and make recommendations independently of the government, although the President would make initial appointments to the council. The panel noted that such a body had first been advocated twenty years earlier by the Commission on Freedom of the Press, headed by Dr. Robert M. Hutchins. A similar recommendation had been made in 1968 by the National Advisory Commission on Civil Disorders.

With much of the media in opposition, the Twentieth Century Fund July 16, 1973 formed a fifteen-member National News Council to monitor media performance and investigate complaints by the public of unfair or inaccurate news treatment. Plans for the council had been announced by the fund's director, M. J. Rossant, November 30, 1972. Its chairman was Roger J. Traynor, former chief justice of the California Supreme Court. It included fourteen representatives of the media and the public. The panel's main function, the fund said, was to investigate complaints against national print and electronic media—the national wire services, the largest supplemental wire services, the national news chains, national weekly news magazines, broadcast networks and public television and radio. Another function was to speak out on "infringements, real and potential, on the right to report the news." A fourteen-member task force, nine of whose members were newsmen, had drafted the proposal.

The creation of such a body had been opposed by a 257-to-106 margin in answers to a questionnaire sent to members of the American Society of Newsaper Editors in the fall of 1972. Support for the council, however, had been voiced by several media representatives who were present when Rossant made the fund's announcement. CBS News President Richard Salant, a member of the task force that had proposed the council, was quoted as saying that "there hasn't been enough examination of what we [the media] do. Take it out of the hands of the people who have an ax to grind—put it into the hands of systematic, independent investigators." CBS later endorsed the council, but the ABC and NBC networks refused to cooperate with it.

The New York Times announced January 15, 1973 that it would not cooperate with the council. *Times* publisher Arthur Ochs Sulzberger wrote in a memo to his staff that the council would only divert attention "from people who are attempting to intimidate or to use the press for their own ends," and would, despite the good intentions of the participating journalists, "encourage an atmosphere of regulation in which government intervention might gain public acceptance." The public has enough opportunity to criticize the media in letters and statements, he said.

John S. Knight, editorial chairman of Knight Newspapers, was quoted later as saying that "any self-respecting editor who submits . . . to meddling by the National Press Council is simply eroding his own freedoms." *The Arizona Republic* warned editorially July 19, 1973 that there are "dangerous moral implications the Council has on First Amendment rights of the press to operate unfettered."

Under some circumstances, inquiry into media performance seems to be favored by media people. In June 1973 the National Press Club made public an analysis by the Communications Department of American University of Nixon Administration relations with the media. The conclusions of the study, in which the press club's Professional Relations Committee joined, included an assertion that "in the long run, debate of any kind seems a sign of health. Anything that is so important to good government as improved reporting should be a matter for national discussion, and the news media should welcome that. It is difficult to argue that their operations in Washington cannot stand more scrutiny and planning. Nor is it to be doubted that the local view of the federal government, which Nixon Administration officials have so passionately sought, must be heard in the press and on television. . . . We found . . . an urgent need for a will on the part of both officials and journalists to seek superior reporting of complex public issues. . . ."

Accuracy: The 10,000 (or 100,000) 'War Resisters'

Domestic opposition to the American war in Vietnam had induced many military-age Americans to flee to Canada (and other countries) in the late 1960s and early 1970s as draft evaders or deserters from the armed forces. These "war resisters" in Canada became an increasingly controversial topic. The media reported frequently and at length on these refugees and their numbers—and thereby added confusion to controversy.

Russel B. Nye, a professor of English at Michigan State University, reported in the *Washington Post* May 9, 1972 on two years of checking he had done into media reports on how many draft evaders and deserters were in Canada. What emerged, he asserted, "is clear evidence of extremely sloppy journalism." The totals reported ranged from less than ten thousand to a hundred thousand. "Most striking," Nye wrote, ". . . was the almost complete lack of plain legwork. I found no journalist who had consulted easily obtainable Canadian immigration figures. . . . Canadian embassy and consular sources will, if asked, estimate about 10,000 American draft evaders in Canada . . ., but nobody asks them."

Nye said he began checking after hearing Martin Nolan of *The Boston Globe* "remark confidently on television" October 24, 1971 that there were "over 50,000 war resisters in Canada." In answer to a written query from Nye, Nolan cited his sources as James Reston, Jr., "who had used the 50,000 figure in *The New Republic* without attribution."

Widely varied totals were uncovered in the media by Nye's further inquiries: In 1968 *U.S. News & World Report* "gave estimates varying from 300-400 to 25,000." *The New York Times* in 1969 used estimates of "several thousand" in April and of sixty thousand in December, then "shifted its estimate [in 1970] to 6,000-60,000 . . . as well as quoting an 'independent estimate of 20,000.' " The figures were sometimes picked up and used in other publications and broadcasts.

In 1971, Nye wrote, "*Newsweek* cited 50,000-70,000," the Toronto *Globe & Mail* "chose 30,000-100,000," and "Mike Wallace on 'Sixty Minutes' used a new Montreal Registers' estimate of 100,000, noting that it was perhaps inflated. . . ." Roger Williams, on different pages of his 1971 book *The New Exiles,* "cited both 40,000 and 60,000 . . . for 1970," Nye reported, and "at the close of his study . . . increased this to 50,000-100,000."

Nye noted that in January 1972 "*Newsweek* led off . . . with '75,000, mostly in Canada,' while David Brinkley . . . made it 75,000-100,000," Gannett News Service used the figure '60,000-100,000' " and "UPI settled on 70,000."

Nye had started his article with the assertion that he had "never really trusted newspapers very much" when it comes to facts. Twenty-five years of historical research had helped convince him "that newspapermen are highly fallible sources of information," he declared. Nye concluded after his two-year check on draft-evader reporting, "I trust the press no more than before, nor do I have any more information than before."

Do Poor People Eat Cat & Dog Food?

Americans were startled in mid-1974 to learn from a June 19 report by United Press International that "in the world's wealthiest country [the United States], as much as one-third of the dog and cat food sold in city slums is being eaten by humans." The shocking report was attributed to "a panel of nutrition experts" and was picked up by publications and broadcast media both in and out of "the world's wealthiest country." Finally, somebody tried to check the report.

Robert W. Samuelson, a Washington writer, disclosed his findings in the *Columbia Journalism Review*, one of the publications specializing in media criticism, and his article was reprinted in the November-December 1974 issue of *Nutrition Today*. According to Samuelson, the sources of the pet-food-for-the-poor report had no evidence to support the widely believed statement.

The UPI had based its report on a single sentence in a 172-page report on government food programs. The report had been prepared for hearings of the Select Senate Committee on Nutrition & Human Needs. The authors of the report were a "panel of hunger experts" headed by Ronald Pollack, director of the Food Research & Action Center in New York City.

Pollock supported the report's assertion by saying, "We know that a lot of people eat dog food." He admitted that it was impossible to verify the claim that poor people ate a third of the pet food sold in city slums, but he absolved his panel of responsibility, noting that his colleagues had merely quoted, unquestioningly, a statement attributed to the Washington-based Center for Science in the public Interest.

The latter group, Samuelson found, reacted with embarrassment. It seems that Michael Jacobsen, a center co-director, was the author a year previously of a short book entitled *Nutritional Scoreboard: Your Guide to Better Eating*. In the book, Jacobson had rated the nutritional value of the dog food Alpo and had found Alpo far more nutritious than such items as McDonald's small hamburger, hot dogs, bacon and bologna. Jaconson was interviewed by a Scripps-Howard reporter when the book was published in July 1973. The last line of the interview, as printed in the July 25 issue of the *Washington Star-News*, said: "Dog food is included, Jaconson said, because one-third of dog food sold in ghettos is reportedly bought by the poor for themselves." Samuelson wrote that Jacobson said he did not remember making this estimate "but concedes that he might have."

With such little verification, the pet-food statement was incorporated in the official staff report of the Select Senate Committee on Nutrition & Human Needs, was repeated by the Pollack "panel of hunger experts" in its report to the committee and so found its way into the press. Samuelson noted that columnist Jack Anderson took this unverified report "one step further: My associate Les Whitten tried some of the pet foods. . . . He found the canned pet foods, though edible, had a rank taste which made him queasy. The dry foods . . . were course tasting and hard to swallow. When he mixed them with water and salted them, they were at least palatable. Peanut butter or cheese spread made dog food easier to get down, he found. But the poor can seldom afford these tasty spreads.' "

Samuelson called it "tempting to dismiss all this as a case of mistaken enthusiasm for a hollow horror story." He asserted, however, that the pet-food angle was "only a little less well-researched [by the media] than other coverage given . . . to the report . . . on federal food programs. . . ."

Bias in Coverage: Sevareid Vs. Solzhenitsyn

The media had been accused of virtually ignoring flagrant Communist brutalities during the fighting in Vietnam but of providing abnormally heavy coverage of atrocities that may have been committed by Americans or South Vietnamese troops.

An example of this was reported by Accuracy in Media in November 1973:

The Soviet dissident writer Alexander Solzhenitsyn had charged in a letter to the Norwegian newspaper *Aftenposten* September 11, 1973 that the Communist massacre of about 3,000 civilians in Hué in February 1968 "had been lightly noticed and almost immediately forgiven" in the West because "the sympathy of society was on the other side." CBS News commentator Eric Sevareid asserted in his television and radio commentary the following evening that Solzhenitsyn "is saying in general that Western liberals tend to excuse the profound inhumanity of Communist regimes. Some do. But this theme of Solzhenitsyn requires some rebuttal. The Hué massacres were heavily reported. Many other brutalities by the North [Vietnamese] were missed or reported sketchily at second hand, simply because we could have no reporters or cameras with the enemy forces."

Chairman Reed J. Irvine of AIM, contesting Sevareid's claim that Hué atrocities were "heavily" reported, wrote to Sevareid that his clipping files show no "heavy reporting of the Hué massacres." On the contrary, the *New York Times* and *Washington Post* reports on the slayings appeared to be scanty and meager. "I would consider it one of the most under-reported stories of the decade," Irving wrote. He contracted this with the coverage of the My Lai massacre by U.S. troops, "an atrocity which did not begin to compare with the Hué butchery." The My Lai story "broke in November 1969," and *"The New York Times Index* for 1969 alone contains three and a half pages of entries (over fifty entries per page) on My Lai plus one page of photos," Irvine noted.

Sevareid, who answered "after some prodding," according to AIM, replied that when AIM "was founded I took it to be . . . an agency designed to focus a politically neutral, objective scrutiny on the media. . . . [I]t has become clear that AIM is . . . ideologically motivated. Its only interest lies in refuting inaccuracies or alleged inaccuracies that reflect adversely on the right wing philosophy, right wing interests and the military establishment. That is why I have not replied to your queries . . . and why I shall not acknowledge your queries or protests in the future."

AIM called Sevareid's message "a totally unjustified attack on AIM, . . . [used] as an excuse for his refusal either to prove that he was right or admit he was wrong." AIM executive secretary Abraham Kalish wrote that AIM's ideology was a belief in "freedom and democracy." This, he held, was not necessarily right wing. AIM, which "depends almost entirely on complaints received about inaccuracies and bias," had "never refused to investigate any complaints of substance," Kalish asserted, "and would not do so on ideological grounds." He called it "surprising that Sevareid should refuse to accept criticism from those who might differ with him politically even if it relates to questions of factual accuracy." Kalish recalled a May 18, 1971 statement by Walter Cronkite, Sevareid's "colleague at CBS," that "we commit errors of fact, and the offended always must have the right to bring us to task when such occurs by sloth or inadvertence." Kalish added that "proven errors should be corrected, regardless of the source of the complaint, since the correction is not for the benefit of the complainant alone but for the benefit of the audience."

AIM also quoted James Jones's assertion in *The New York Times Magazine* of June 10, 1973 that the Hué battle "received enormous publicity in America in 1968, but the aftermath (the massacre) didn't. . . . Some pieces were written about it in

America but dropped from sight quickly. . . . And it was not until November 1969, when a Nixon speech [mentioned Hué], . . . that the subject got additional attention in the press. But at that time, few American reporters saw fit to take it on. . . . Hué was no longer news. Anti-U.S. feeling was high at home. Why buck it in the cause of unpopular truths? Much better to concentrate on our own rottenness at My Lai."

Years earlier, Sevareid himself had spoken out on a need for better news broadcasts that should include the airing of objections to items on the broadcasts. To do "a markedly better job" and provide "better balance," he said in the Fourth Annual Elmer Davis Memorial Lecture at Columbia University April 29, 1970, network news programs should "go to an hour's length. . . . In that hour we could do what we should always be doing, in my long sustained opinion; we could provide room for rebuttals to our practices from ordinary listeners; letters to the editor, if you wish. For years the situation has cried out for this. . . ."

Failure to Inform the Public

The media is frequently accused of failing to report important news. Some complaints may be self-serving charges by people with a political, ideological or economic ax to grind. But many journalists as well as apparently disinterested observers also say that developments of vital concern to the public are commonly ignored by the media.

An annual media research project—Project Censored—is conducted at Sonoma State University in Rohnert Park, Calif. to determine "The Best Censored Stories" of the year. The term *censored* in this instance is a harsh substitute for *overlooked* or *ignored*. The 1979 report is an example of the project's controversial findings. Under the direction of Carl Jensen, associate professor of sociology, a sociology seminar class in mass communications in 1979 selected twenty-five noteworthy stories that had "received little or no mass media coverage in 1978." A panel of twelve prominent jurors was asked to pick from these items the ten "best censored stories of 1978." Jensen said, "We feel the lack of coverage given to a number of significant issues comprises a form of media censorship which has been overlooked in the past."

Performance of the Media

The prominent jurors were journalist Ben H. Bagdikian; Stewart Brand, editor and founder of *The CoEvolution Quarterly* and *Whole Earth Catalog*; Robert Cirino, an author and teacher; David Cohen, president of Common Cause; Nicholas Johnson, former FCC member; Robert MacNeil, executive editor of the Public Broadcasting Service's "MacNeil/Lehrer Report", writer-lecturer Victor Marchetti; syndicated columnist Mary McGrory; writer-lecturer Jessica Mitford; Jack L. Nelson, professor of social education at Rutgers University; educator Joseph J. Schwab, and author-TV personality Sheila Weidenfeld.

The Number 1 "censored" story of 1978, cited by all of the jurors, was the failure to inform Americans of the potential dangers of nuclear power. The Union of Concerned Scientists had been trying for years to explain these hazards. In 1978 this public interest group issued a report headed "Scientists' Group Judges Federal Nuclear Safety Inspection Effort," but, Project Censored asserts, the media largely ignored it. "It is not surprising that many Americans were shocked by what happened at Three Mile Island," Jensen said, "since the media had not told the public what a strong possibility there was for such a disaster."

The other nine "best censored stories," in order, were:

Organic farming. Daniel Zwerdling reported in *The Progressive* (in "Curbing the Chemical Fix: The Secret Is It Works") that commercial organic farmers have been successful with the alternative to chemical pesticides that are said to cause cancer, birth defects and other health problems.

War on scientists. According to an article ("The Government's Quiet War on Scientists Who Know Too Much") in a March 1978 issue of Rolling Stone, scientists who uncover uncomfortable facts may be harassed by the government. Example: Dr. Thomas Mancuso, working on a 1964 Atomic Energy Commission contract, turned up evidence that low-level radiation might endanger workers in nuclear plants. His contract was cancelled and he lost his research funds.

U.S. exports death: The Third World asbestos industry. The U.S. Government clamped down stronger regulations for the asbestos industry after researchers showed in the 1960s that asbestos-plant workers who inhale asbestos fibers increase their risk of cancer. The media, however, did not inform Americans that instead of improving plant safety, asbestos manufacturers moved their factories to such tolerant Third World countries as Mexico,

Taiwan, South Korea, India and Brazil. They thus increased their profits because of low wages and exported the cancer risks to foreign workers.

Winter choice: heat or eat. The Citizen/Labor Energy Coalition reported in November 1978 that thousands of Americans had to choose between paying high fuel bills or spending their scarce funds on food, rent or medicine. More than 200 deaths in the winters of 1975-77 were linked to discontinuation of gas and electric service to homes.

America's secret police network. Few Americans were told by the media about the Law Enforcement Intelligence Unit (LEIU), a private organization that links the intelligence squads of most major U.S. and canadian police forces. Its members are state and city police officers, but LIEU is not responsible to official organizations nor subject to freedom-of-information law. Its files are said to be more secret than those of the FBI and CIA.

The specter of sterility. Another poorly told story is that of the substantial decline in the sperm count of American men in the past thirty to fifty years. The probable cause is the wide use of industrial and farm poisons.

Dangerous dams. It is reported—but not widely by the media—that the safety factor was often overlooked in the building of the 49,422 large dams around the United States. Some twenty-five to thirty of them may break in any given year, estimates Dr. Bruce A. Tschantz, University of Tennessee civil engineering professor and White House consultant on dam safety. About 39,000 of them have never been inspected by state or federal authorities.

Nutrition and mental illness. Mental illnesses may often be caused by diet deficiencies, according to investigators. It is asserted that proper nutrition could help 6,400,000 of the Americans receiving mental care and an additional 13,600,000 who need such care. Abram Hoffer, physician and biochemist, reports that seventy per cent of convicts jailed for serious crimes suffer from vitamin deficiencies that lead to aggresive behavior. He adds that vitamin deficiencies or low blood sugar were found in ninety per cent of convicted murderers diagnosed as paranoid schizophrenics. One to five million schoolchildren diagnosed as hyperkinetic are suffering toxicity from food dyes and flavors, estimates Benjamin F. Feingold, chief emeritus of the Kaiser Permanente Department of Allergy. Yet the least funded area in nutrition research is said to be mental health. Despite the importance of these findings, they are largely overlooked by the media.

Who owns America? Maurice Zeitlin, in an article in *The Progressive,* rejects the assertions that the financial situation of most Americans is improving, that "the economic class system is disappearing." Zeitlin cites statistics tending to show that "the same old gang" still owns America. In 1860, the wealthiest one per cent of the population owned twenty-four per cent of the nation's wealth, according to economic historians cited by Zeitlin. In 1969, the wealthiest one per cent owned 24.9 per cent. According to an *Editor & Publisher* article on 1978's "best censored stories," "the myth of economic progress is another continuing media deception."

The Sonoma State University researchers deny that the "censorship" of stories such as these is a product of some media "conspiracy." Instead, they suggest, the failure to report such significant developments is traceable to lack of knowledge or understanding or to such motives as profit, the media's identification with big business or an unwillingness to rock the boat.

Although the medium had been criticized as failing to inform the public adequately about the dangers of atomic energy, the newspapers and broadcasters were later praised for a largely responsible job of journalism following the March 1979 accident at the Three Mile Island nuclear power plant in Pennsylvania's Susquehanna River Valley. An investigation of the entire incident was made by the President's Commission on the Accident at Three Mile Island. It reported to President Carter October 30 that "while the media can be criticized for missing some stories and failing to provide a context for others, they were generally not guilty of the most common criticism leveled at them: that they presented an overwhelmingly alarming view of the accident." "The media generally attempted to give a balanced presentation which would not contribute to an escalation of panic," the commission reported. "There were, however, a few notable examples of irresponsible reporting, and some of the visual images used in the reporting tended to be sensational."

The commission said it had examined the coverage of the accident by 43 newspapers and had found sensationalism in only *The New York Post* and the New York *Daily Times*. Neither of the two criticized papers agreed with the commission's charge.

Balance: Reporting the Cambodian Holocaust

The media has been accused by some sources of shamefully inadequate coverage of mass slaughters by the Communist regime of Pol Pot in Cambodia. Critics have suggested that this alleged inadequacy was especially indecent when contrasted with heavier coverage of lesser atrocities in rightwing countries.

Former Nixon speechwriter Patrick Buchanan reported in *TV Guide* March 18, 1978 on the media's treatment of a Washington press conference January 20 by Pin Yathay, a Cambodian civil engineer. Yathay had escaped from Cambodia after twenty-six months of horror during which he had lost his eighteen-member family. He reported on torture, executions, suicides and starving people practicing cannibalism.

All three networks were invited by the American Security Coucil to attend the Yathay press conference, Buchanan wrote, but "not one sent a correspondent." He reported that the *Washington Post* reporter (Elizabeth Becker) walked out midway, "asserting that she had heard enough of this 'junk'," and only syndicated columnist Jack Anderson put the story on network television—on "Good Morning America."

By comparison, Buchanan said, "both ABC and CBS ran extended stories" January 2 on how South Africa editor Donald Woods fled his country after being banned from publishing there, and NBC January 6 gave heavy coverage to "Woods' escape, his family's harassment, his scathing judgment of South African justice." "ABC, which could not send a correspondent three blocks to hear Pin Yathay in Washington," sent "Issues and Answers" personnel three thousand miles to London to interview Woods, Buchanan wrote.

Accuracy in Media checked into the *Washington Post*'s treatment of the Yathay press conference. AIM reported that, according to Miss Becker, it was *Post* national news editor Laurence Stern who decided not to print anything about it. Questioned by AIM, Stern said he had "decided not to do a story" because Miss Becker had said the Yathay material was similar to material being reported by Lewis Simon, *Post* correspondent in Bangkok. AIM checked and asserted that "we could not find in all the previous year a single news story in the *Post* that provided a detailed eyewitness account of the incredible treatment of the Cambodian people comparable to that provided by Pin Yathay." It was ten months since the *Post* had printed anything by Simon on the subject, AIM reported, and the point of his article was that "accounts of a bloodbath had been exaggerated, but there were severe problems because of a crop failure and disease." AIM again checked with Stern, who replied that he had been thinking of earlier stories—in 1975 and 1976.

According to AIM, the *Post*'s own tabulations showed four articles on the topic in 1976 and nine in 1975. "The longest story the *Post* ran on Cambodia in 1977," AIM reported, "was a two-page article making the charge that Cambodia's plight was really the fault of the U.S. for having gotten Cambodia involved in the war. Two articles were devoted to defense of their policies by Communist Cambodian leaders, and even the articles that discussed the agony of the Cambodian people tended to be 'balanced' by mention of U.S. culpability or arguments that things were not as bad as some said."

In his 1978 article ("The Power of the Press: a Problem for Our Democracy") in *Policy Review,* Max Kampelman wrote that reports on the "plight of the Cambodians . . . [had] appeared regularly over the French news wire services, dating from the Khmer Rouge guerrillas' capturing of the country. The American daily press, however, until recently, largely ignored the modern-day holocaust in Cambodia." Kampelman noted the *Wall Street Journal* suggestion that Communist atrocities in Cambodia had excited less media attention than less significance inhumanities elsewhere "because they are inflicted in the name of revolution." "Massacres and mass executions in many Third World countries have warranted only a few paragraphs, if anything," Kampelman asserted, whereas rock-throwings or a single killing in Israeli-controlled areas evoke "front-page news stories and photographs." He conceded the irony that some of the disproportionate coverage was due to the fact that free countries permit press reporting of such events whereas the media is excluded from unfree nations and therefore cannot cover "a slaughter in Cambodia or the training of terrorists in Libya."

A charge frequently made by rightwing critics is that Communist influence—or at least liberal bias—in the American media may be the explanation for such media behavior as the treatment of the Cambodian horrors. The November 1979 issue of the rightwing *American Opinion* clearly made such a charge. John Rees, in an article entitled "Washington as Censored by the *Post*," reported that following Laurence Stern's death August 11, 1979, "a great deal was ... revealed ... by the circle of his admirers...." *Village Voice* columnist Alexander Cockburn was quoted as writing: " ... Larry's heart and head lay on the left side of the political bed. He was not one of those pallidly objective souls who ... feel incapable of making up his mind 'until all the facts are in' and till all the evidence has been judiciously assessed. A Trotskyist in his hot youth, Larry knew what the facts were going to tell him long before he discovered that they actually were ... "

Rees wrote that "distortion is not always caused by the deliberate efforts of a reporter or editor to misrepresent the facts. It can also involve something now called the 'Pinsky Principle'." This "principle" bears the name of Mark Pinsky, a North Carolina free-lance journalist. Pinsky, in a 1976 article for the *Columbia Journalism Review*, analyzed the press treatment of the trial of Joan Little, who was charged with murdering her white jail guard. Her defense was that she had killed him in self-defense during a rape.

"The great untold (or unreported) story of the John Little trial," Pinsky asserted, " ... was the role of the Communist Party, through its National Alliance Against Racist & Political Repression, in controlling the entire (and considerable) political movement surrounding the case." Although Communist "party members were visible and influential on the defense committee, and the party frequently set up rallies of support around the country," Pinsky wrote, "straight reporters did not report this situation, out of a concern that the information might be used in red-baiting anyone associated with the case who did not belong to the party." The "Pinsky Principle," the reason Pinsky himself and other reporters are said to have decided not to report important information, was summed up by Pinsky thus: "If my research and journalistic instincts tell me one thing, my political instincts another, ... I won't fudge it, I won't bend it, but I won't write it."

Staging & Distortion of News & Documentaries

In 1971 Representative Harley O. Staggers (Democrat of West Virginia), chairman of the House Interstate & Foreign Commerce Committee and of its Sepcial Subcommittee on Investigations, discussed allegations made to his panel that material intended for broadcast sometimes is "staged" or deliberately distorted by television personnel. In one case, it was reported, CBS had planned to stage and film an invasion of Haiti.

"It has been alleged," Staggers said April 20, 1971, "that various broadcasters in connection with the preparation and/or presentation of purportedly *bona fide* news programs and documentaries have engaged in practices which might result in misleading and deceiving the public. These practices include: (1) Prearrangement or 'staging' of events which are then presented as though they were *bona fide* and spontaneous news storeis; and (2) production techniques, including the manipulation of sound tracks, film and/or videotape, which rearrange the sequence of events, mismatch responses given during interviews, or otherwise distort the actual event originally filmed by the camera."

Staggers reported that Congress, "and this subcommittee specifically," had examined a number of the allegations. "In some significant instances," he declared, "the allegations were determined to be well-founded in fact." One of the programs involved was the documentary "Pot Party at a University," prepared and presented by station WBBM-TV of Chicago. Another was "Hunger in America," a CBS News documentary. Staggers said his subcommittee had also examined "in detail the production of a CBS documentary which attempted to follow the adventures of a group seeking to invade the island of Haiti and overthrow its government. This was, of course, the much discussed 'Project Nassau.' This documentary was never brought to final completion or broadcast. . . . "

Elsewhere (*e.g., Barron's,* March 29, 1971) it was alleged that in the case of "Project Nassau," CBS actually "sought to stage, and to film," the invasion of Haiti; this allegation was denied by CBS. The same source (*Barron's*) reported that in the "Hunger in America" documentary, the CBS narrator said of a baby shown: "This baby is dying of starvation. He was an American. Now he is dead." "Untrue," asserted *Barron's.* "The baby was born prematurely and, according to an FCC report, died of 'septicemia due to meningitis and peritonitis'."

The Staggers subcommittee "found that fraudulent and deceptive production techniques had been used in producing 'Project Nassau,' " Staggers declared. He reported that CBS, 'both at the time and since, has asserted that its activities were a legitimate exercise of 'news judgement'." The Staggers panel, rejecting this argument, asserted that "fraud and deception in the presentation of purportedly *bona fide* news events is no more protected by the First Amendment than is the presentation of fraud and deception in the context of commercial advertising or quiz programs."

"To the average viewer," the Staggers subcommittee said in its "Project Nassau" report, " . . . a network news documentary typically represents a scrupulously objective reporting of actual events shown as they actually transpired. If 'Project Nassau' is any indication, this is not always true. During the preparation of this news documentary, CBS news employees and consultants intermingled and interacted with personages actively engaged in breaking the law. Large sums of money were made available to these individuals with no safeguards as to the manner in which these funds would be put to use. Events were set up and staged solely for the purpose of being filmed by the CBS camera. . . . . Rather than responding to any taint of artificiality or fraud in the considerable volume of film which had been prepared, the decision [to abandon the documentary] was apparently made on the basis that the project was journalistically unsatisfactory in view of the unfinished nature of the enterprise."

After Vice President Spiro Agnew criticized CBS for allegedly "financing a secret and illegal invasion of Haiti," CBS News President Richard S. Salant issued a reply: "We did *not* finance the planned invasion. We did nothing illegal. No significant amount of money even inadvertently found its way to persons involved in the invasion plan. The Department of Justice found *no* unlawful activities on the part of CBS News. And John Davitt, chief of the Criminal Division of the U.S. Department of Justice, said, quote: 'CBS advised us of the facts, advised the Bureau of Customs that they were there, and that they were filming these episodes.' And at one point the Treasury Department asked us *not* to withdraw from the project. But the short answer to the Vice President is that he is attacking a journalistic investigation that never became a broadcast about an invasion that never took place."

Staggers recalled that in 1959, during hearings on falsification in "quiz show" broadcasts, CBS President Frank Stanton had testified that "the test in every case must be whether any substantial number of the viewing audience is likely, in the given circumstances, to be deceived or misled as to the true nature of the program being offered. That test requires the exercise of human discretion in applying a 'rule of reason.' " Staggers noted that Stanton made this statement about "staged and deceptive quiz programming presented for the amusement of television viewers." He suggested that the Stanton test should be "at least equally applicable to news programming which is presented to the viewers as a basis upon which they are to make political and social decisions . . . which affect their own welfare and the future of this nation." Staggers called it his subcommittee's "view . . . that the American public is entitled to know whether what it is seeing on the television screen is real or simulated, edited or unedited, sequentially accurate or editorially rearranged, spontaneous or contrived."

Dean Burch, then chairman of the Federal Communications Commission (FCC), asserted October 1, 1971, at the "freedom of the press" hearings of the Senate Subcommittee on Constitutional Rights, that "a charge of distortion or staging of the news" was virtually impossible for the FCC to handle. "For example," he said, "we may get a complaint of news distortion based on the claim that the facts of some matter are different from those presented over the air. We have absolutely refused to act there. Very simply stated, deliberate distortion cannot be established by determining what is 'true' and then comparing it with what was broadcast. The Commission is not the national arbiter of 'truth.' Similarly, when a person quoted on a news program complains that he very clearly said something else, the Commission cannot investigate and weigh the credibility of the newsman and the interviewed party. We refer the matter to the licensee [the broadcasting station] for its own investigation and appropriate handling." Nevertheless, Burch held that "staging or slanting the news is flagrantly contrary to the public interest. Indeed, it is difficult to imagine a more effective way to destroy the public's ability to understand and participate in public affairs and thus to destroy the very essence of democracy. . . . "

Max Kampelman wrote in his 1978 *Policy Review* article that the practice of a "new journalism" (and "advocacy journalism" as well as "personal journalism" variations) had this result: "to an unprecedented extent, the media . . . have stimulated, sometimes created, and even actively participated in . . . events" on which they reported. The "new journalism" theory, according to Paul H. Weaver in an article ("The New Journalism and the

Old—Thoughts After Watergate") in the Spring 1974 issue of *The Public Interest,* is (as cited by Kampelman) that the press's responsibility is "to discover truth, not merely facts." The "new journalism" variations, Kampelman added, encourage the reporter "to indicate and further his point of view in his news stories. Objectivity is ridiculed as being impossible to attain."

Distortion: The Bishop's 'Anti-Abortion Sermon'

Controversy is frequently caused by reports of speeches and interviews that distort the intent of a speaker by inflating his remarks or by quoting them out of context. This type of complaint was a major reason for the controverys over "The Selling of the Pentagon." Another controversy of this nature involves Bishop James S. Rausch, who was incorrectly reported in the press to have told then-President Gerald R. Ford "from the pulpit it is his duty to oppose abortion."

As general secretary of the National Conference of Catholic Bishops, Rausch had delivered a Red Mass in Washington January 26, 1975 for the administration of justice. President Ford and Chief Justice Warren Burger attended. Rausch's 1,500-word sermon was devoted to the five human rights that the Synod of Bishops in Rome had listed in 1974. These are the rights to life, to food, to justice, to political freedom and to religious freedom. Exactly five words in the entire sermon referred to abortion: in the right-to-life section (which also discussed such topics as euthanasia, the arms race, torture), Rausch said that "abortion directly attacks this right." At no time did he address Ford or the other officials, although he asserted that the listed areas of rights "merit the serious attention of all of us who are charged with leadership in our time."

The United Press International reported the story on its wire that afternoon under a lead that began: "President Ford attended a traditional Red Mass for justice at Washington's St. Matthew's Cathedral and heard a Roman Catholic bishop tell him from the pulpit it is his duty to oppose abortion." The article reported that "the bishop . . . said Frod, Burger and the other officials sitting in the cathedral must 'assume a responsibility [to defend the human rights] we dare not fail to meet'." (Rausch did not use the word "assume" but did say that the United States, as the world's greatest food producers, had "an awesome responsibility.") The Associated Press report said that Ford and Burger heard the bishop "preach" that abortion " 'directly attacks' the human right to survive" and that Rausch "offered a prayer for the protection of 'unborn children'."

Charles E. Seib, associate editor and "ombudsman" of the *Washington Post,* reported these developments in the February 6 issue of the *Post* and added that the *Post*'s own coverage of the event January 27 was "a rewrite of the two wire service stories, mainly UPI's." It began: "President and Mrs. Ford attended the annual 'Red Mass' . . . yesterday and heard Bishop James Rausch . . . deliver a strong anti-abortion sermon. Claiming that abortion 'directly attacks' the human right to survive, Rausch said the nation's leaders must 'assume a responsibility' to oppose abortion."

"Thus," wrote Seib, "a quarter-hour sermon with a five-word reference to abortion had become an 'anti-abortion sermon' and the country's 'awesome responsibility' in the world food crisis had become a responsibility of our leaders to oppose abortion. So far neither the UPI nor *The Post* has acknowledged the distortion of the bishop's sermon. The next day the UPI transmitted a story quoting an official Catholic denial that the sermon was aimed at the President, but with no comment on its original story." The *Post* printed a letter in which Rausch explained the context of his remarks and denied any demand that the President act. Seib also noted "that similar distortions appeared on television and in other newspapers. . . . "

Seib called it "important to recognize that there was no malice, no intention to deceive or mislead in the handling of the Rausch story. . . . " "Nevertheless," Seib said, "the public was misinformed and an already sore issue [abortion] became a little more inflamed."

Three weeks later Seib printed a comment from Pulitzer Prize-winning journalists Malcolm "Mike" Johnson, who wrote: "Don't tell me that UPI didn't know exactly what it was doing. It was just another case of a wire service stretching the facts to the outer limits, and beyond, in order to get a grabbing, sensational lead. . . . "

Media Surrender to Propagandists?

Among complaints about the media is the charge that is allows itself too easily to be misused for political propaganda.

For example, it is said that terrorism is often aimed almost entirely at media coverage. According to the *Encyclopaedia of the Social Sciences* (1933), the "cardinal point in the strategy of terrorism" is the "publicity value of the terrorist act." It is often argued, therefore, that the media actually encourages terrorism by guaranteeing to provide the publicity that is its purpose. Walter Laqueur asserted in the November 1976 issue of *Harper's,* in an argument repeated a year later in his book *Terrorsim,* that the media acts "as a selective magnifying glass," providing "inordinate publicity" that inflates the significance of the terrorist act. He held that most observers of terrorism realize that terrorists are publicity seekers who play up to the media. "[T]he terrorist act alone is nothing," he wrote. "Publicity is all."

Terrorism, however, is only an extreme example of political activity that entices the media. Media attention is solicited for political activity ranging from election campaigning to demonstrations for civil rights or against nuclear power. The legitimacy of media behavior comes into question when the media appears to encourage riots and other acts of political violence by virtually assuring them of coverage.

The case of Iran is cited by some critics as an example of the American news media serving the purpose of anti-American political activists. The media gave heavy but apparently normal coverage to an important story: the actions of the Islamic revolutionaries and their aged leader, the Ayatollah Ruhollah Khomeini, as their attacks on the Pahlevi monarchy brought about the departure of the shah in early 1979 and the creation of a chaotic revolutionary regime. The media's interest in events was understandably intensified after armed revolutionaries seized the American embassy in Tehran and imprisoned more than half a hundred American embassy personnel as hostages. American television crews soon presented television viewers across the United States with the spectacle of blindfolded American hostages being herded before jubilant Iranian crowds. American television audiences watched representatives of the hostagetakers make long, bitter denunciations of the United States and justify the imprisonment of diplomatic personnel in seeming violation of international law. According to critics of the media, at least some of the demonstrating and American-baiting took place solely because American television provided a forum for enemies of America.

One of the potential coups for which many media people then hungered was an interview with the Ayatollah Khomeini, whose word appeared to be paramount in Iran. Finally, all three American television networks were granted interviews. The three separate interviews took place the same day—November 18, 1979. As demanded by the Ayatollah, all three networks violated their own news policy by submitting their questions in advance. The Ayatollah answered only the questions he wanted to answer. Other questions were ignored. And the Ayatollah used the interview to present his case to the American public.

The networks were criticized for abandoning policy on the demand of a foreign interview subject, and all three networks defended their decisions to do so. Robert Chandler, CBS-TV's public affairs director, said that "what it came down to was: do we get an interview with the Ayatollah or don't we?" CBS and the other networks permit the news president to override the policy if the "news importance of the interview clearly outweighs the disadvantages of the procedure."

At ABC, Stan Opotowsky, director of television news coverage, rejected criticism that the Ayatollah had used the networks. "We always go after public figures in any story, and they always say what they want to say," he declared. "You've got a major story, and he is the major architect of that major story, and it would be journalistically irresponsible not to try to see him and not to report what he had to say."

Ed Planer, NBC vice president for news coverage, had a similar answer. "The Ayatollah is central to the whole story," he said. "Here's a guy who's suddenly become a very important figure in this whole thing, and we have to find out what makes him tick."

Senator S. I. Hayakowa of California was one of the critics of the networks. In a letter to all three, he said, "Your network has interviewed Khomeini under ground rules you certainly would not accept from an American official, allowing him complete control over the interview so that he can be sure that his views are presented without challenge."

Hayakawa asserted in his letter that Khomeini "is just as skillful as Hitler in his use of the media. Morning, noon and night we see the news from Iran on our television screens, and it's usually the same—chanting, cheering crowds of Iranians burning the American flag and effigies of our President. . . . " "I wonder what would happen," he asked, "if American networks stopped paying so much attention to the Ayatollah and his gangs? . . . The purpose of television is to bring us the news—not propaganda. I believe that without the encouragement of television cameras, the demonstrations in Iran would slow down and stop . . . . I am not suggesting that freedom of the press should be interfered with in any way. Of course, the American people have a right to know and should know what is going on in Iran. But it seems to me that the Iranians are using the media in an effort to hypnotize the American public with dramatic, exotic, violent images to the exclusion of rational discussion. . . . ."

Seducing the Media

One of the ethical questions that trouble members of the media is the common practice of "free-loading" by news people. Free trips, payment of hotel and restaurant bills, entertainment, gifts, discounts for merchandise and sometimes even expense money are routinely provided by representatives of business or government who quite obviously hope that their largesse will result in favorable publicity.

A minority of broadcasting firms and publications try to solve the problem by forbidding employees to accept some or all of these "courtesies." Others permit the free-load with the explanation that their news people are professionals who use "free-bies" to help them do their job but who would not let it influence them when they write.

The issue received an unusually wide public airing January 23, 1974 when it was explored on the CBS program "60 Minutes." The program opened with interviewer Mike Wallace describing a scene in the Smokey Mountains of North Carolina: "Thirty automotive news reporters . . . who write about the cars we buy are setting out to test the new Cherokee jeep. . . . [What they] write about a car can make a million dollars difference in sales. . . . Almost all these reporters had their air fare and their hotel bills paid for by American Motors, the compnay that makes the jeep. . . . Only two or three hours of the time the reporters spent in North Carolina were devoted to testing the Cherokee. The rest went to drinking, eating and being entertained."

Wallace reported that "most of the reporters saw . . . nothing wrong with American Motors picking up their tabs." "They never pressure me," said one reporter. "I think the rules are pretty well recognized by both the companies and the writers," said another. Frank Hedge, American Motors vice president for public relations, defended the junkets as, according to Wallace, "legitimate and routine." "There's no attempt made to force them to write anything," said Hedge, "because we're too sophisticated to think you can force a writer to write against his better judgment."

But Paul Poorman, managing editor of the *Detroit News,* opposed free-bies. After heading an Associated Press managing editors group that studied the subject, Poorman said, "I don't think that newspapers should do this [permit junkets]. . . . It's dishonest. . . . We're supposed to be as objective as possible about it [the topic on which they are reporting], and you can't be objective when you're being entertained by someone else." He told Wallace that "it doesn't really matter if you know that you're implicitly honest and doing the right thing if somebody else is convinced that you're not, becuase that perception becomes the reality. We're in a fairly cynical, almost hostile, public environment. Nobody belives anything anymore, to generalize, and it's important that they believe us. And if they don't believe us, we're useless."

Wallace pointed out that "press junkets are standard practice in most of the automobile industry," as they are in other industries. Among things not well known to the public, he continued, was the fact that "most of the top local sportscasters in this country not only have their travel bills paid for them by the team they cover, but also their salaries. . . . " Other free-bies range from foreign travel to football tickets, to "lavish Christmas gifts," to parties. He cited Paul Poorman as saying his staff had been offered "courtesies" worth over $100,000 in a single year. An AP managing editors study showed that two out of three of them said they would accept free trips; one out of two would accept free overseas trips; and gifts were found acceptable by three out of four. Even Poorman, who opposed free-bies and whose *Detroit News* now barred them, said he had once received a discount of several hundred dollars when he bought a car before his paper made acceptance of discounts a firing offense.

Wallace reported that CBS, his own network, forbids CBS employees to go on junkets. But he said that CBS public relations people arrange junkets for television critics, who suggest in their articles what TV shows their readers should watch. "Like the other networks," Wallace said, "CBS regularly flies television reviewers to New York or California on expense-paid trips to look at new network productions and to meet network personalities."

Press attaches of foreign governments also arrange free trips for reporters who want to do stories in the countries they represent. Wallace noted that when personnel from NBC's "Today" program spent a week in Rumania and another in Ireland, the Irish and Rumanian governments and Pan American Airways paid for their air fare and hotels. "When 'Today' travels overseas, all their expenses, over and above their normal budgets, are paid for by the host country," he said.

Wallace, who no longer accepts free trips, said that he also had gone on junkets in the past. In a survey of well-known journlists, he found that those who said they would not accept junkets included Joseph Alsop, Evans and Novak, Joseph Kraft, Shana Alexander, Mary McGrory, David Brinkley, John Chancellor, Howard K. Smith, Harry Reasoner, Carl Rowan and Eric Sevareid. Those who at that time acknowledged having gone on junkets "in recent years" were Martin Agronsky, Milton Viorst, the late Bob Considine, Charles Bartlett. Walter Cronkite and William Buckley—"all of whom scoff at the notion that their reporting can be bought."

Broadcasters Under Pressure

Regulating Radio & Television

The federal government licenses broadcasting stations. The print media remains unlicensed, largely because the First Amendment forbids "abridging the freedom . . . of the press." Dean Burch, then chairman of the Federal Communications Commission (FCC), explained October 20, 1971 at the "freedom of the press" hearings of the Senate Subcommittee on Constitutional Rights: "Government licensing of newspapers has been and continues to be abhorred in this nation because the power to license carries with it the threat of government control of news . . . "

The distinction between newspapers and broadcasting stations, and the reason that, according to Burch, "the government must license broadcast stations," was stated by the Supreme Court in 1943 in the case of *NBC* v. *United States*. In a decision that applies to television as well as to radio, the court held: "Unlike other modes of expression radio is not available to all. That is its unique characteristic, and that is why, unlike other modes of expression radio is not available to all. That is its unique characteristic, and that is why, unlike other modes of expression, it is subject to government regulation." The number of radio frequencies or television channels is limited, and the FCC assigns the available rights among competing applicants under a licensing scheme embodied in the Communications Act of 1934, as amended. Licenses are awarded to serve the "public convenience, interest, and necessity." If a licensee fails to perform this service, the FCC can revoke or refuse to renew the license.

The Communication Act's "comprehensive scheme for regulating the use of radio [and television channels] in the larger interest of the public is not inconsistent with the First Amendment," Burch held. "This is not because the First Amendment is inapplicable to radio—the protections of the First Amendment certainly do apply to broadcasting. The Supreme Court has so stated on several occasions; Section 326 of the Communications Act so states. Rather, government regulation is permissable because different standards are appropriate for different media of expression in light of their differing natures. Thus, since radio is inherently not available to all, regulation of the use of radio in the public interest does not violate the First Amendment."

Chief Justic Warren Earl Burger, in his last opinion as an Appeals Court Judge (in the case of *Office of Communications of United Church of Christ* v. *FCC* in 1966), held that "a broadcaster has much in common with a newspaper publisher, but he is not in the same category in terms of public obligations imposed by law. A broadcaster seeks and is granted the free and exclusive use of a limited and valuable part of the public domain; when he accepts the franchise it is burdened by an enforceable public obligation. A newspaper can be operated at the whim or caprice of its owner, a broadcast station cannot."

"The first obligation of the broadcaster," Burch said, "is to engage in broadcast journalism—to devote a reasonable amount of time to informing the public on controversial issues of public importance," and the FCC, therefore, had "allocated a relatively large amount of spectrum space to this service." To justify this allocation, the Supreme Court ruled (in the case of *Red Lion Broadcasting Co.* v. *FCC* in 1969) that broadcasters must act "as proxies for the entire community, obligated to give suitable time and attention to matters of great public concern. . . . " (The court said in this decision that "a license has no constitutional right . . . " to monopolize a radio frequency of his fellow citizens. . . . ")

The FCC, Burch asserted, had "stressed the need of the licensee to discharge this obligation by presenting partisan voices, rather than 'always itself presenting views in a bland, inoffensive manner.' " Such a presentation policy by a licensee, the FCC held, would run counter to the Supreme Court's view (in *Times Co.* v. *Sullivan* in 1964) that there was a "profound national commitment that debate on public issues be uninhibited, robust, and wide-open debate."

"In line with that objective," Burch reported, "the Commission believes that the broadcaster cannot properly present only one side of the debate—the side with which he agrees. The Commission, therefore, early developed the fairness doctrine as a necessary corollary of the public interest standard of the Comunications Act. The doctrine emerged in a series of early cases and then was enunciated in considerable detail as the result of a proceeding initiated by the Commission to clarify its position with respect to the obligation of licensees in the field of broadcasting news commentary and opinion. . . .

"Simply stated, the fairness doctrine requires that where a broadcaster has covered one side of a controversial issue of public important, he must afford reasonable opportunity for the discussion of contrasting viewpoints. He cannot sit back and wait for someone to knock on his door and offer to present the other side. He must affirmatively encourage and implement the presentation of other sides. . . . In presenting other viewpoints, the broadcaster has considerable leeway to make good faith, reasonable judgments as to the viewpoints to be presented, the appropriate spokesmen, the format of the program, and many other similar programming decisions. Thus, fairness, that is, affording 'reasonable' opportunity does not mean the mathematical precision of 'equal' opportunities—a concept which is applicable only to broadcasts by legally qualified candidates. The Commission's role in enforcing the fairness doctrine is limited. The Commission determines, upon appropriate complaint, whether the broadcaster's judgment can be said to be unreasonable. The Commission does not . . . determine whether it is a wise journalistic judgment or one with which this agency would agree."

The fairness doctrine as outlined by Burch was codified in the 1959 amendments to the Communications Act. Section 315(a) requires licensees " . . . to afford reasonable oportunity for the discussion of conflicting viewpoints on issues of public importance." During the 1960s the FCC also adopted the rules applying to personal attacks and to political editorials. These rules require a broadcaster to give, in Burch's words, "timely notification to a person or group attacked and to the candidate opposed or not supported and to make an offer of comparable time for a response."

The above rules and the general fairness doctrine were challenged, largely on First Amendment grounds, in the *Red Lion* case. In upholding the FCC and the fairness doctrine, the Supreme Court said in 1969 that "there is no sanctuary in the First Amendment for unlimited private censorship in a medium not open to all. Justice Byron White, writing for the court, asserted that "there is nothing in the First Amendment which prevents the government from requiring a licensee to share his frequency with others and to conduct himself as a proxy of fiduciary with obligations to present those views and voices which are representative of his community and which would otherwise, by necessity, be barred from the airwaves." The court held, however, that the First Amendment "has a major role to play" in broadcasting, a role recognized by Congress when, in Section 326 of the Communications Act, it forbade the FCC to interfere with "the right of free speech by means of radio communications."

"Because the scarcity of radio frequencies, the government is permitted to put restraints on licensees in favor of others whose views should be expressed on this unique medium," the court said. "But the people as a whole retain their interest in free speech by radio and their collective right to have the medium function consistently with the ends and purposes of the First Amendment. It is the right of the viewers and listeners, not the right of the broadcasters, which is paramount. . . . It is the right of the public to receive suitable access to social, political, esthetic, moral, and other ideas and experiences which is crucial here. That right may not constitutionally be abridged either by Congress or by the FCC."

FCC Commissioner Nicholas Johnson also testified at the Senate "freedom of the press" hearings October 20, 1971 and declared himself largely in agreement with Burch's views. In an amplification of the rationale for government regulation of broadcasting, Johnson said: "The radio spectrum and the right to broadcast were considered a national resource, owned by the people as a whole. In deciding how that national resource was to be used, . . . [it] was not given to private users, nor was it sold. . . . Congress determined that private licensees would be chosen by the FCC to operate stations as fiduciary trustees of the American people as a whole. Private profit would be permitted, but Congress clearly contemplated that non-remunerative programming would also be required. The public was thought to be entitled to a public service in exchange for the profitable use of its property. . . . The act expressly spells out that a broadcaster does not own a license in the way that a newspaper owns its 'right' to print."

Broadcast journalism leaders rejected the FCC and Congressional justifications of government regulation of the electronic media. Larry H. Israel, chairman of the board of Post-Newsweek Stations, expressed some of the principal anti-regulation views April 27, 1972 in a speech at the University of Missouri's School of Journalism. "Precisely the same checks and balances which have served for almost two centuries to protect us from abuses in print journalism will protect us from abuses in broadcast journalism," he declared. " . . . One of the more significant holdings of the Supreme Court has been interpreted by some as meaning that the First Amendment exists not to protect broadcasters but to protect the public. But it is essential to go one additional step to ask whether it is *possible* for the public to be protected *unless* broadcast journalism—like newspaper journalism is free from any form of government influence or coercion." The answer of "the reformers," Israel said, is that "television and radio are *different*. . . . Broadcasters must be tightly regulated, goes the argument, because they are making use of scarce public resource. But . . . is this really true? Newspapers, magazines and other means of wide and general circulation are even more scarce. Here in Missouri, in St. Louis and Kansas City, for example, there are substantially more TV and radio stations than daily newspapers. Does it then follow that regulation should be extended to other media as well, because of scarcity? To the contrary, it means that the underlying rationale for government supervision of broadcast journalism is faulty and that broadcast journalism should be as free as any other journalism."

"As always," Israel warned, "we come back to the fundamental choice: private judgments or government judgments. Totalitarian societies depend on government involvement in and control of ideas and information. Free societies . . . depend utterly on the much-more-risky business of allowing ideas and information to bounce around in the open marketplace. . . . " "Curiously and tragically," Israel asserted, broadcasting, "the medium which evolved . . . [in] recent history into the most effective communications medium of all time, has been subjected to increasing government oversight in the exercise of its journalistic role." This took place at a time, he said, when "the censorship which has restricted public dialogue on sensitive political issues has retreated steadily as the courts have enlarged the scope of the First Amendment."

Another leader of broadcast journalism, NBC news commentator Bill Monroe, warned February 24, 1973 that acceptance of government curbs on the electronic media could result in pressure for curbs on the print media as well.

Addressing the Minnesota Newspaper Association, Monroe recalled hearing a newspaper city editor end a telephone argument "with a politically powerful city councilman by telling him to go to hell" and hanging up. "He was a newspaperman, and he had a deep sense of security about his independence from government," Monroe pointed out. "My experience in broadcasting . . . is that broadcasters do say no to the politically powerful, but, even if provoked, they just don't allow themselves the luxury of strong language. You don't have that sense of security in an organization that's got to get a government okay every three years to stay in business. . . . The station managers tell their news directors to go ahead and air the news stories offensive to politicians. But they feel a compulsion at the same time to worry about the possible backlash. . . . Regulation of editorial content builds in a timidity factor. . . . And once you've accepted the value of government guidelines for one medium, the idea that such guidelines provide net benefits to the public, then you've quit really believing in the First Amendment. . . . You're on the way toward the next step . . . : having improved one medium by government guidelines, to set about improving other media the same way. If government can make television news fair and balanced, it can make newspapers fair and balanced. . . . "

Fairness Doctrine Reconsidered—and Reaffirmed

A three-year reconsideration of the fairness doctrine was begun by the Federal Communications Commission in June 1971. This study culminated in an announcement by the FCC July 3, 1974 that, because of "the need for the fairness doctrine," the commission had "reaffirmed its position that 'strict adherence' to the doctrine is the 'single most important requirement of operation in the public interest' and an absolute necessity 'for grant of a renewal of license.' "

The FCC reported that there were two fundamental considerations prompting its reexamination of the fairness doctrine: "First, in view of the profound unquestioned national commitment embodied in the First Amendment, our goal in this area must be to foster 'uninhibited, robust, wide-open' debate on public issues." The second consideration (based on the first) is the maintenance and growth of a broadcast system compatible with the public interest. "It is axiomatic," the FCC said, quoting from its 1949 "Report on Editorializing," "that one of the most vital questions of mass communication in a democracy is the development of an informed public opinion through the public dissemination of news and ideas concerning the vital public issues of the day."

The FCC, in reaffirming the fairness doctrine, conceded that "At first appearance, this affirmative use of government power to expand broadcast debate would seem to raise a striking paradox, for freedom of speech has traditionally implied an absence of governmental supervision or control. Throughout most of our history, the principal function of the First Amendment has been to protect the free marketplace by precluding governmental intrusion." A different approach was taken, the FCC said, in view of the evolution of the mass media technology and the "concentration of control." "This approach—an affirmative one—recognizes the responsibility of government in maintaining and enhancing a system of freedom of expression," the commission declared.

The broadcaster's problems with the fairness doctrine are illustrated to some extent by the case of the September 1972 airing of NBC-TV's documentary "Pensions: the Broken Promise." The FCC rule December 3, 1973 that the program, critical of private pension operations, had violated the fairness doctrine. The decision upheld a complaint by Accuracy in Media that the program conveyed the "distorted and propagandistic" impression that "failure and fraud are the rule in the management of private pension funds" but ignored "the great achievement of American private enterprise in developing a pension system that is overwhelmingly successful."

NBC was given the option of complying with the FCC's ruling by programming "positive" material on private pension operations on its network newscasts. NBC declined to accept this option. Instead, it appealed the FCC ruling to the federal Court of Appeals. It warned that the decision would have a potentially destructive effect on television's abillity to broadcast investigative programs. In its arguments before the FCC, NBC had charged the commission staff with error in extending the fairness doctrine into news judgment. NBC pointed out that the program was not a pro- and-con survey of the pension system but an investigative documentation of the system's problems. The network added that, even so, the program included documentation of positive aspects of pension plans.

NBC's appeal was upheld September 27, 1974 by a three-judge federal appeals court in Washington. In a 2-1 ruling, the court voided the FCC's decision and the requirement that NBC broadcast material showing favorable aspects of pension plans in order to counteract the effect of the original program. The appeals panel upheld the validity of the fairness doctrine but held that "editorial judgments of the licensee mustn't be disturbed if reasonable and in good faith." Especially in regard to investigative journalism, the court ruled, the FCC was not to tamper with a broadcaster's judgment unless the commission could show clearly that "the licensee has been unreasonable and that there has been an abuse of journalistic discretion rather than an exercise of that discretion." In cases involving investigative reporting, such as this one, the court held that there was the "greatest need for self-restraint" on the part of the FCC and "keen awareness" by the commission of the inhibitive effect of government intrusion. The court noted that its decision was based largely on the "misapplication" of the fairness doctrine in a specific case rather than on broader First Amendment claims of press freedom.

As in other cases of programs under attack, "Pensions: The Broken Promise" had been widely supported and praised. It had received a George Peabody Award for public service in television (the citation called the program "a shining example of constructive and superlative investigative reporting"), a Christopher Award (for "television news calling public attention to a much-neglected social issue"), a National Headliner Award and a Certificate of Merit of the American Bar Association.

Senator William Proxmire of Wisconsin, in a renewed attack on the fairness doctrine, told the Senate August 5, 1974 that he considered "the so-called fairness doctrine" a violation of "the spirit and letter of the First Amendment"—despite the fact that "the Supreme Court has on several occasions upheld the constitutionality of the doctrine." "Any restriction on the news function of broadcasting is an abridgment of the free press," he declared.

" . . . The licensing of broadcasting is an abridgment. When licensing is predicated on that which is broadcast, that, I belive, is manifestly a diminution" of freedom of speech and of the press.

Network Power Investigation Started but Suspended

In early 1977 the FCC began a controversial study of allegedly undue domination of the television industry by the three major broadcast networks, but the inquiry was suspended indefinitely within six months, ostensibly because Congress was withholding the money needed for the investigation.

The investigation had been proposed in a Westinghouse Broadcasting Company petition that was upheld by the Department of Justice November 23, 1976. The department called on the FCC to inquire into the "structure, power and affiliate relationships" of the National Broadcasting Company, CBS, Inc. and the American Broadcasting Companies. The department suggested that the FCC "address the possibility" that the networks be required to divest themselves of some or all of the stations that they owned or operated.

"Given their combined market share and current levels of profitability," the department said in its brief, "network control over owned and operated stations may well contribute importantly to the networks' ability to preempt program acquisition and, consequently, to distribute a disproportionate share of programming and to obtain a disproportionate share of broadcast revenues." Such activity by the networks, at the expense of their affiliates, "would raise serious issues both as a matter of communications policy and of antitrust policy," the department's brief said. It posed the possibility, according to the brief, that the "great economic power" of the networks "may have substantially eroded the ability of affiliated licensees to exercise genuine independence in making programming decisions."

All three major networks opposed the recommended investigation. CBS said the Justice Department-Westinghouse arguments were "without merit." ABC said they were lacking in substance and based on unwarranted "inferences." NBC held that the department's concern for the Westinghouse petition was "misdirected" because, it said, the petition "ignores the needs of the many affiliated stations in small markets across the country for network economic and programming support."

The FCC January 14, 1977 agreed to make the investigation. Issues it found worthy of study included the questions of: (a) whether local stations affiliated with the networks were obliged to sacrifice their independent judgment on the programs they carried because of contractual arrangements with the networks (according to different estimates, from 75 percent to 85 percent of the 700 commercail television stations in the United States were affiliated with the three major networks); (b) whether network compensation of the affiliates was influenced by the amount of programming the affiliates agreed to carry; (c) whether the networks, through their control of production facilities, had frozen out competition from independent program producers; (d) whether the affiliates had adequate time and opportunity to preview network offerings before agreeing to run them, and (e) whether network ownership of television stations had adversely affected the quality and quanitity of syndicated program offerings. The FCC, however, decided not to inquire into whether the networks should be required to divest themselves of the stations they owned and operated.

By June 30, 1977, the investigation was apparently over. Outgoing FCC Chairman Richard E. Wiley said the inquiry was being suspended indefinitely because a Senate Appropriations subcommittee had decided to withhold the money needed for the investigation. Democratic Senator Ernest F. Hollings of South Carolina, the subcommittee chairman, was said to have opposed funding the probe until the White House appointed successors to Wiley and another departing FCC commissioner, Benjamin L. Hooks.

Separate antitrust suits had been filed earlier against the three major networks. In actions entered December 10, 1974, the Justice Department had accused the networks of using their control over access to network air time to restrain and monopolize prime-time television entertainment programming. Similar charges had been filed against the networks in April 1972, but the case had been dismissed in November 1974 "without prejudice." The networks had claimed that the 1972 suits had been filed as part of a vendetta by the Nixon Administration. A Justice Department spokesman denied this claim. He said the charges were based on findings from an investigation that had begun in the 1950s and had been suspended during the period 1959-70 while the FCC conducted hearings on network programming. NBC sought to settle in 1977. In a consent decree approved by the federal court in Los Angeles December 1, NBC agreed to restrict its television production activities and its agreements with independent producers. Much of the settlement, however, was to take place only if the other networks also settled, and, initially, at least, both CBS and ABC resisted.

Government Rules Eased for Radio

Modifying a series of proposals originally made in 1979, the Federal Communications Commission voted January 14, 1981 to eliminate some of the important restrictions on radio broadcasters. The 6-1 decision (a) ended the requirement that stations maintain detailed logs of their programming and commercials, (b) allowed stations to broadcast as many commercials per hour as they desired, (c) eliminated the requirement that stations devote a specifice minimum percentage of their air time to news or public affairs programs, and (d) abolished the formal procedures that stations had been required to observe in finding out the broadcast needs of their communities.

Untouched, however, were the rules requiring stations to comply with the fairness and equal-time doctrines, to serve the public interest, to avoid discriminating against women and minorities and to apply for license renewal every three years.

The lone dissenting vote in the FCC decision was cast by Tyrone Brown, the FCC's only black commissioner, on the ground the relaxation of rules was too broad. Brown, whose resignation from the commission took effect January 20, won the FCC's agreement to a requirement that every radio station file a list of five to ten issues of community interest that it had covered in its programming. The list would be reviewed by the commission when a station's license was challenged.

FCC Chairman Charles D. Ferris explained that as a result of the relaxation of regulations radio broadcasters would no longer have to "follow empty governmentally required procedures and compile stacks of paperwork. Instead, they will be able to follow their own path in determining how to serve their community's needs and interests in ways that reflect the realities of today's radio markets." A spokesman for the Media Access Project, a Washington-based public-interest group, denounced the change, however, with the complaint that it was a "sad day for minorities, women, the poor, religious groups and other working people who have relied on the FCC to make sure that radio stations meet the needs of the listeners they serve."

Ownership & Control of the Media

Newspapers and broadcasting stations are such obvious sources of power that they exert a virtually magnetic attraction on many ambitious people. It is easy to see that access to the opinion-forming facilities of the print and electronic media can shorten the route to domination in government, politics and business and can make retention of power more certain.

Yet the American newspaper, an institution older than the nation, was able to survive until the Twentieth Century before its independence was challenged by publishing chains and conglomerates and its influence by the upstart radio and television. The broadcast media, children of this century, came under the domination of the network system almost from birth despite legislation that limited multi-station and cross-media ownership.

Fewer Newspapers, Concentration of Ownership

The independent American newspaper, according to many newsmen and other observers, has become an endangered species. The number of papers has been declining for at least half a century, and the ownership of the surviving publications has been concentrated increasingly in the hands of fewer publishers.

"Our press is fast evaporating," civil-liberties attorney Morris L. Ernst wrote in 1946 in *The First Freedom*. "Ten states have not a single city with competing daily papers. . . . Three hundred and seventy chain newspapers own about one-fifth of our circulation. There are only 117 cities left, in our entire nation, where competing dailies still exist. . . ." Thirty-three years later, in an address in mid-1979, editorial page editor Millard C. Browne of the *Buffalo Evening News* commented on Ernst's lament: "[L]ittle did he [Ernst] know. Today . . . we have not 117 cities with competing dailies but only thirty-four such cities. And today we have chains owning not one-fifth of all daily circulation but three-quarters."

The situation was described by John B. Oakes, former editorial page editor of the *New York Times,* as he delivered the Frank E. Gannett Memorial Lecture at the Washington Journalism Center May 17, 1978. "As the capital investment required to produce and publish newspapers has increased," Oakes said, "three distinct but related economic developments have taken place." These are "the formation of 'media conglomerates' linking under one ownership a wide variety of large enterprises; the establishment of enormous newspaper and broadcasting chains; and the development of both conglomerates and chains into publicly held stock corporations." Oakes held that there is a major fear on the part of those who criticize "the growing concentration of power in the news industry in the hands of relatively few communications companies." This fear is that "the more concentrated power becomes, the more likely it is to move the focus of print journalism away from its original goals and purposes into becoming a mere money machine, as has happened in the television industry."

At the same time, many newspapers ceased publication because of increased costs and the resulting inability of many cities to support more than one paper. In an effort to reduce legal barriers to more efficient newspaper operation, Congress passed the Newspaper Preservation Act July 8, 1970, and President Richard M. Nixon signed it July 24. The law exempted from antitrust treatment certain Joint Operating Agreements between failing and successful newspapers. It permitted the joint operation of production facilities but continued the prohibition on the merger of editorial staffs and policies. In effect, the new law provided antitrust exemption for newspapers alredy operating in twenty-two cities under such agreements. The Department of Justice, which had opposed the law, was authorized to provide antitrust exemption for new agreements under the act.

There were other critics of the law aside from the Department of Justice. Peter Barnes charged in the October 17, 1970 issue of *The New Republic* that this "masterful piece of special-interest legislation," "whisked through Congress under great pressure from powerful newspaper publishers," was "like a license to operate an unregulated monopoly." "The immediate beneficiaries," he wrote, included such publishers, "not exactly paupers," as Randolph Hearst, Samuel Newhouse, John Knight, the Mormon Church and the Scripps-Howard organization as well as "several independent publishers who own radio and TV stations, cable television interests. . . ."

The growing concentration of media ownership has serious First Amendment implications. Marvin L. Stone, editor of *U.S. News & World Report,* addressing the American Association of State Colleges & Universities in 1977, noted that "the Founding Fathers enacted the First Amendment in large measure to protect journalistic diversity from government encroachment." "But diversity may now be imperiled," he warned, "and ironically, not by government but by the dynamics of the marketplace. Great and venerable publishing enterprises are under pressure to join chains or conglomerates for a safer existence alongside goods ranging from rental cars to rugs."

Another concerned observer, Maurice Rosenblatt of Washington, discussed the situation in February 1979 at the St. Regis Conference in Luxembourg. "New York City, in 1920, had fifteen daily newspapers," he said. "In 1963 there were still twelve. Today there are three. Across the country, in 1910, there wre 2,202 daily newspapers, all but sixty-three indepently owned. By 1977 the total number had dropped to 1,762, of which 1,047 were owned by groups." Rosenblatt added that "the large chains are now buying up smaller chains." He cited "a valid projection . . . that within two decades virtually all of America's daily newspapers will be owned by fewer than two dozen communication conglomerates." "The one-newspaper town has become the rule," he declared.

Larry Pressler, then a Republican Senator-elect from South Dakota, expressed concern December 22, 1978 that "the First Amendment is being threatened by the fact that a small handful of people have ultimate control over many of our media and publishing outlets." In a letter to Griffin Bell, then Attorney General,

Pressler asserted that "such conglomerates as CBS; Time, Inc.; Dow-Jones; Knight-Ridder; Gulf & Western; Gannett; Newhouse; Scripps-Howard . . . are examples of media conglomerates that are nearly pure monopolies in our society. Not only do they publish huge chains of newspapers, but they also have cross-ownership of other media outlets—including polling firms, book distribution networks, pulp mills, timber land, record distribution groups . . . and other activities that are not necessarily directly related to publishing." Pressler noted that "1984 is just five years away. If the present trend continues, over eighty per cent of American newspapers will be chain-owned. . . ." He added that "other communications conglomerates are allowing a very small number of people to have ultimate direction over what books are distributed, what appears on national television, and what moves over national news and financial wires." Pressler suggested that Department of Justice action under the anti-trust laws might be the way to correct what he saw as a threat to press freedom.

Assistant Attorney General John H. Shenefield of the Anti-Trust Division, replying on the Attorney General's behalf, wrote to Pressler March 7, 1979 that "we all would prefer more news sources to fewer but . . . the anti-trust laws do not flatly prohibit media conglomerates. . . ." He said that "despite the number of recent newspaper mergers, even the largest of the newspaper chains accounts for only a relatively small percentage of total daily circulation. For example, in 1977 the newspapers owned by Gannett represented approximately only 4.7 per cent of total daily newspaper circulation in the United States." Shenefield added that even when a city had only one newspaper, the publication, "whether or not it is chain-owned, is not entirely free from competition from other media. Thus, it may be accurate to view it as operating in a broader anti-trust market that includes such other media." The causes of the decline in the number of cities with competing newspapers, he said, "include economies of scale as well as increased competition from alternative advertising media such as suburban daily and weekly newspapers and television. Anti-trust enforcement, in addition to seeking to preserve the remaining direct daily newspaper competition, is also concerned with preserving competition between daily newspapers and these other media."

Defenders of the media *status quo* have suggested that, since the number of large and medium-sized newspaper chains exceeds at least fifty, the threat of monopoly in the press field is not as serious as that in, for example, the automobile industry, where only three or four significant American auto makers were then in competition with each other and with foreign imports. Media critic Ben. H. Bagdikian pointed out in the June 1978 issue of *Progressive* magazine, however, that the auto makers do compete with each other—and do so throughout the country. No comparable competition exists among the media conglomerates. Bagdikian noted that "the Gannett chain, which had seventy-six papers the last time I looked, does not compete with Lord Thomson's fifty-six papers or with Knight-Ridder's thirty-two papers or with Samuel Newhouse's thirty papers." The newspaper chains, he asserted, "are secure systems of local monopolies, effectively insulated from competition with each other."

Millard Browne, in a mid-1979 address, expressed an opinion quite different from Shenefield's. "Growing concentration of newspaper ownership," he said, "does equal monopoly in an astonishingly high proportion of the local markets where newspapers in this country flourish—and where they used to compete. Of the 1,760 dailies published in about 1,600 American communities, there is only one local newspaper company in 97.5 per cent of those communities."

Browne quoted Bagdikian's comment at a Federal Trade Commission "Workshop on Media Concentration" that "it took the first sixty years of this century for chains to control twenty-seven per cent of all out papers. It has taken only the last sixteen years for chains to reach control of sixty-one per cent of all papers and seventy-five per cent of all daily circulations." All the other mass media are affected by the phenomenon of "fewer and fewer people controlling more and more of our public intelligence," Bagdikian said, and, according to Browne's citation, "fewer than one hundred corporate executives . . . [have] ultimate control of the majority of each media" in the country. Bagdikian found that "fifty-two per cent of all daily newspaper sales" was controlled by twenty corporations; fifty per cent of all periodical sales was also controlled by twenty corporations, as was fifty-two per cent all book sales and seventy-six per cent of all record and tape sales. Counting the three networks and ten major sponsors, "thirteen corporations control two-thirds of the audience in TV and radio," Bagdikian asserted, and "seven corporations control seventy-five per cent of movie distribution." Overlapping ownership actually reduces the number of such controlling corporations to less than the total of controlling firms in each medium.

A further reason for the concern about concentration of power in the news industry is the fact that, as Bagdikian pointed out in his *Progressive* article, "our daily newspapers are still the dominant source for all news in the United States." The broadcasting networks do not have news bureaus in all large and medium-sized cities. Most of the news reported in most of the media "comes overwhelmingly from the two wire services," the Associated Press and United Press International. The wire services, however, do not originate all the news that they pas on to the media. Instead, they get most of it from the country's daily newspapers, a source that at the same time constitutes their rosters of local members and clients.

Bagdikian called attention both to the concentration of newspaper ownership and to a "qualitative difference in the social impact of media conglomerates" and of other conglomerates. When a conglomerate uses its newspaper to benefit another of its subsidiaries, "that is dishonest news," he asserted. With chains and their wide interests, he suggested, "when contamination of the news occurs, it can be on a massive scale."

Nashville Newspapers Change Owners

In what became a perhaps enlightening series of events regarding the issue of newspaper chains and conglomerates, John Seigenthaler testified May 24, 1979 before the Senate Select Committee on Small Business as publisher of the *Nashville Tennessean,* which he described as "an independent newspaper," "In a real sense, Seigenthaler said, "I have not been concerned about the trend toward chain ownership because I know and trust most of the people who direct and manage chains and those who publish and edit their chain-owned papers. They have motives that are good. They know this industry. They want the best for their papers."

Segenthaler, however, expressed "fear that the future of our industry will include secret manipulations by those vast conglomerate managers who can see immense profits and unprecedented power in corporate control of the press." He said he worried that the newspaper industry would be hit by proxy fights and tender offers, that the chains ultimately might be controlled by "the oil and energy conglomerates, the huge banking-insurance holding companies, or shadow operators," and that "the integrity of the press would suffer." "Who can trust the conglomerate-holding company view of First Amendment responsibility?" he asked. "The ultimate question . . . is whether a free press, in publicly held chains, may not become a contradiction in terms."

In his prepared testimoney, Seigenthaler described the situation then in Nashville, a two-newspaper town: His paper, the *Tennessean,* had "been owned independently since 1937 by the Evans family. . . . Since that year, it has been part of a Joint Operating Agreement with the *Nashville Banner,* currently owned by the Gannett chain. . . . The Joint Operating Agreement, which is validated by the Newspaper Preservation Act, has meant that there would be two separate editorial voices in our readership area and that there would be competition for news—even though the business affairs of the newspapers were carried on in the same manner as it is conducted in so-called 'one-newspaper towns' . . . .My own first-hand views and my chief impressions of chain-operated newspapers are perceived largely through my focus of the *Banner's* management by Gannett since 1972. As one who has worked all my professional life for the same Evans family-owned newspaper, I have strong, visceral preferences in favor of locally controlled dailies. . . . Beyond that personal preference, I am concerned about the many implications of where concentrated control is taking the American press. . . . I think it is a mistake, viewing Gannett's ownership of the *Banner,* to sugges that my concerns abouit chain ownership have anything to do with . . . 'quality journalism.' The *Banner* is a different paper under Gannett ownership; by standards acceptable to most news consumers, it is a better paper."

Seigenthaler asserted, however, that "if our city has gained a more readable afternoon paper with the coming of the Gannett, it also has lost something perhaps intangible that goes with local independent ownership." The local owner displaced by Gannett "knew his city, loved it and . . . dedicated his paper to it," Seigenthaler said. "The roots of his paper were buried deep in the soil of Middle Tennessee. It saddens me that those roots have been taken up and transplanted in Rochester [Gannett's headquarters]." He said it was probably "too late to question whether the movement to chain-ownership by publicly held corporations is inexorable." He called it "certainly too late to question whether monopoly ownership in a local community is good or bad. That is reality...."

Less than two months later, in what the Wall Street Journal described July 9, 1979 as "an unusual move," Gannett arranged to sell the *Banner* and buy the *Tennessean,* retaining Seigenthaler as president, publisher and editor. Under antitrust law, Gannett could not own both papers in the same city. The new owners of the *Banner* were a local group headed by John Jay Hooker Jr., who had been an unsuccessful Democratic Party candidate for governor.

Domination of Broadcasting

Regular licensed broadcasting was started in 1920. Scheduled network broadcasting began a scant two years later when the American Telephone & Telegraph Company (AT&T) arranged a telephone hookup of its station WEAF in New York City and station WNAC in Boston.

Network leadership—or domination—of broadcasting followed quickly. The AT&T planned its first coast-to-coast broadcast in mid-1923 with a Presidential address from San Francisco. The plan had to be abandoned because of the illness and death of the President, Warren G. Harding. A seven-station network was put together that fall, however, to broadcast the convening of Congress, and Calvin Coolidge's 1925 inaugural address was broadcast over a network of 26 stations. By this time radio stations were also organizing themselves into networks for advertising purposes.

Even at this early stage, there was competition for control of the airwaves. The Radio Corporation of America (RCA) challenged AT&T by using Western Union telegraph wires for a radio network, but these facilities proved to be unsatisfactory. The Westinghouse Corporation and RCA also experimentat with shortwave radio as the medium for a network. This too was less than successful.

Ultimately, the competitors came to an agreement. RCA, the General Electric Company and Westinghouse were to share the ownership of a single radio network—the National Broadcasting Company (NBC). The independent stations of the network were to be tied together by the use of AT&T telephone lines. And AT&T agreed to sell its New York radio station WEAF to RCA.

Ownership and Control of the Media 115

The NBC network was an immediate success. Business was so good that it split into two NBC networks—the Red network and the Blue—in 1927, and it soon controlled virtually all major programs.

Such power and success, however, could not remain long without challenge. A new network, the United Independent Broadcasters—now the Columbia Broadcasting System (CBS)—was put together before the decade had ended. Under the young William Paley, who became CBS president in 1930, a startling innovation took place when all CBS stations were cleared for a live broadcast of a disastrous fire in Ohio State Penitentiary. The screams, agonized sobs, ambulance bells and crackling sounds of flames were forerunners of the tragic events that were soon brought from scenes of war and disaster into the homes of radio listeners and—not very much later—television viewers.

Television broadcasting came hard on the heels of radio. As RCA's David Sarnoff asserted, television technology was already "an accomplished fact" in the 1920s. By 1931 an actual television program was broadcast by CBS on an experimental basis. World War II interrupted television's progress—but only briefly. Television came along with a rush after the war, and it soon dominated broadcasting. Radio became a relatively dim companion to the new electronic star.

Meantime, in the late 1930s, the Federal Communications Commission began to look into the matter of network domination of broadcasting. After three years of investigation, the FCC ruled in 1941 that no corporation would be allowed to own more than one network. NBC had to sell off one of its networks, and the Blue network ultimately became ABC (the American Broadcasting Companies). The three "major" networks—NBC, CBS and ABC—are still considered the dominating factors in commercial broadcasting.

Marvin L. Stone, in his address before the American Association of State Colleges & Universities, discussed the dominating role played by the three networks in television, "the electronic medium that has reshaped American society." Conceding that "it takes vast resources to bring a moonwalk into our living rooms" and that "small, independent television enterprises could not offer much of the excellent news and public affairs programming the networks provide," Stone added that "the networks also give us much inferior fare" and that "there is little choice for viewers outside the offerings of the Big Three." Stone asserted that "quality is secondary to profits" in the network view. "They worship at the altar of the Ratings God," he said, "and as a result, all too often what they pipe into our homes is raw sewage, polluting our minds." He pointed out that "the networks are all part of giant conglomerates" with diverse interests. He asked whether it is "desirable for these firms—whose most important mission should be to inform the public—to have interests that could come into conflict with that mission? Is it good for society to have networks owned by large conglomerates which treat TV as just another product to be merchandized? Does it make sense to have television dominated by only three corporations? . . ."

Meanwhile, the FCC had been looking into another aspect of domination of broadcasting. After a two-year study, the commission decided March 26, 1970 to prohibit any new combination in which the same proprietor would own more than one broadcasting station—radio or television—in the same city. In granting new licenses, the FCC said, it would observe a "single market" rule "designed to prevent undue influence on local public opinion by relatively few persons or groups." Exceptions were made for: (a) Owners of limited-power AM radio stations in communities with 10,000 or fewer residents; such owners would be permitted to acquire FM radio stations in the same market. (b) Owners of daytime-only Am stations; they would be able to acquire FM stations in the same market area. (c) Owners of AM-FM radio combinations seeking to sell; they would be permitted to sell both outlets to a single buyer if they demonstrated that the stations could not be sold to separate buyers for economic or technical reasons.

At the time of this order, according to an FCC report, 256 daily newspapers in the United States were owned by holders of broadcast licenses in the same city. In sixty-eight relatively small communities, a single proprietor owned both the only daily newspaper and the only commercial radio station. In eleven cities, the only television station and the only daily newspaper were owned by the same proprietor.

In 1975 the FCC broadened its attack on media domination by barring transactions through which new combinations of newspaper and broadcasting ownership would be created in the same market. More than 140 such combinations then existed. The commission order permitted all but twenty-three of them to continue. The twenty-three cross-media operations ordered to dissolve were in communities in which the only newspaper and only radio or television station were in the hands of a single owner. They involved seven newspaper-television combinations and sixteen newspaper-radio ones. (FCC jurisdiction was in the broadcast area and did not extend to newspapers not involved in cross-media operations. Anti-trust law, however, barred monopolization of newspapers in all but one-newspaper towns.)

Acting on a challenge to the 1975 FCC order, the United States Circuit Court of Appeals for the District of Columbia ruled March 1, 1977 that the ban on simultaneous ownership of a newspaper and broadcasting station in the same market area must be expanded to include existing as well as proposed combinations. The appeals court decision, however, was reversed by the Supreme Court June 12, 1978. The high court, in an 8-0 ruling, upheld the FCC's order, including the "grandfather" arrangement allowing most existing newspaper-broadcasting combinations to continue.

Broadcasting-station and newspaper owners had sued to have the FCC order invalidated. The Department of Justice and the National Citizens Committee for Broadcasting, a public-interest group based in Washington, D.C., went to court also in an effort to have the FCC order broadened by requiring that all existing newspaper-broadcasting combinations be dissolved. The commission opposed the break-up of most of the combinations on the ground that this would cause reductions of news and other expensive programs by impairing local ownership or management, disturbing "continuity of ownership" or causing "local economic dislocations." The appeals court, ruling unanimously for the Department of Justice and the National Citizens Committee, held that the FCC had been mistaken in seeking "to limit divestiture to cases where the evidence discloses that cross-ownership clearly harms the public interest." Instead, it said, divestiture should be required "except in those cases where the evidence clearly discloses that cross-ownership is in the public interest."

Supreme Court Justice Thurgood Marshall, author of the decision that overturned the appeals court ruling, held that the ban on future cross-media combinations—but not on all existing ones—was "a reasonable means of promoting the public interest in diversified mass communications." Citing the Supreme Court's *Red Lion* decision of 1969, Marshall asserted that there is no "unbridgeable First Amendment right to broadcast comparable to the right of every individual to speak, write or publish. . . . A newspaper need not forfeit anything in order to acquire a license for a station located in another community."

Democratic Congressman Lionel Van Deerlin of Calfornia, supporting the "grandfather" arrangement, explained to the House of Representatives Sept. 23, 1980 that "the trend of ownership in broadcasting in the United States was . . . greatly influenced in the early years by a reluctance among many potential independent operators to apply for broadcast licenses—and this was especially true when television licenses became available in the early 1950s—because of the tremendous costs involved. In the face of these conditions, the Federal Communications Commission was itself involved in persuading a good many newspaper publishers in the land to acquire licenses, so as to get stations on the air—to begin the very costly operations which, in early days, were substantially supported out of newspaper profits. In more recent times it became far likelier that a television station, out of its profits, is supporting the newspaper that was its progenitor. . . ."

Libel Laws as Media Curbs

Libel is generally described as unjustly, untruthfully defamatory communication that tends to expose its victims to public contempt. Modern libel laws are designed to protect people from unfair damage to their reputations by libel. These laws are descended, as Thomas I. Emerson notes in *The System of Freedom of Expression* (1970), from actions once taken "primarily to protect the government against criticism or to prevent breach of the peace by persons . . . in defense of their honor." Such laws quite clearly are in conflict with the First Amendment's guarantee of freedom of the press.

The unconditional defense to a charge of libel is that the communicated assertion is provably true. Over the years, the authority of libel law has been increasingly circumscribed by the courts in decisions based on strict interpretation of the dictate of the First Amendment. Groups and organizations have been denied relief under libel law. Judges, legislators and government officials are granted immunity to libel action for statements involved in the performance of their official duties. The media can report official documents and proceedings and make "fair comment" without fear of libel action.

Public Officials Limited in Right to Sue

A landmark decision against libel laws was made in the case of *New York Times* v. *Sullivan* in 1964, when the Supreme Court ruled unanimously March 9 that the First Amendment "prohibits a public official from recovering damages for a defamatory falsehood relating to his official conduct unless he proves the statement was made with 'actual malice'—that is, with knowledge that it was false or with reckless disregard of whether it was false or not."

The decision reversed a $500,000 libel judgment awarded by Alabama courts to L. B. Sullivan, commissioner of public affairs (police) in Montgomery, Ala. The award was against *The New York Times* and four black ministers—Ralph Abernathy, Fred L. Shuttlesworth, S(olomon) S. Seay, Sr., and J. E. Lowery. The case was based on alleged libel in an advertisement published in the *Times* March 29, 1960 by the Committee to Defend Martin Luther King and the Struggle for Freedom in the South. The four ministers were officials of the committee. Several inaccuracies appeared in the advertisement. (E.g., the advertisement said that "after students sang 'My Country, 'Tis of Thee' on the State Capitol steps, their leaders were expelled from school. . . ." The students actually sang "The Star Spangled Banner." Those expelled were punished for demanding service at a lunch counter, not, as the advertisement implied, for the demonstration on the Capitol steps.)

Justice William J. Brennan, Jr., in his majority opinion, said that Sullivan could seek a new trial if he thought he could prove "actual malice." According to Brennan, however, the *Times*' "negligence" in failing to discover the factual errors in the advertisement was "constitutionally insufficient to show the recklessness that is required for a finding of actual malice."

The ruling asserted that the case must be considered "against the background of a profound national commitment to the principle that debate on public issues should be uninhibited, robust, and wide-open, and that it may well include vehement, caustic and sometimes unpleasantly sharp attacks on government and public officials." "Neither factual error nor defamatory content suffices to remove the constitutional shield from criticism of official conduct," the court said. It warned that "the pall of fear and timidity imposed upon those who would give voice to public criticism is an atmosphere in which the First Amendment freedoms cannot survive."

Brennan asserted that "erroneous statement is inevitable in free debate and . . . must be protected if the freedoms of expression are to have the 'breathing space' they need . . . to survive. . . . A rule compelling the critic of official conduct to guarantee the truth of all his factual assertions—and to do so on pain of libel judgments virtually unlimited in amount—leads to . . . 'self-censorship.' Allowance of the defense of truth, with the burden of proving it on the defendant, does not mean that only false speech will be deterred. Under such a rule, would-be critics of official conduct may be deterred from voicing their criticism, even though it is believed to be true and even though it is in fact true, because of doubt whether it can be proved in court or fear of the expense of having to do so. . . ."

Justice Hugo L. Black issued a separate opinion that an "unconditional right to say what one pleases about public affairs is . . . the minimum guarantee of the First Amendment." Justice Arthur J. Goldberg also issued a separate opinion that likewise opposed a "malice" test for freedom of expression. The First Amendment, he asserted, gave "to the citizen and to the press an absolute, unconditional privilege to criticize official conduct despite the harm which may flow from excesses and abuses." This right to speak about public officials and affairs should not depend upon a probing by the jury of the motivation of the citizen or press," he said. Justice William O. Douglas joined both Black and Goldberg in their separate opinions.

Media's Protection Broadened

New York Times v. *Sullivan* was followed by a series of decisions that further broadened the media's protection against libel action. "At the present time," wrote Columbia Law Professor Alfred Hill in "Defamation and Privacy under the First Amendment," an article in the December 1976 issue of *Columbia Law Review*, "media defendants cannot be held for defamation of public officers or public figures except for misconduct that is willful or reckless (the *Sullivan* rule); and cannot be held liable for defamation of private persons, or of public persons in their private capacities, except upon a showing of 'fault,' which probably is satisfied by proof of negligence. . . ."

Not all libel controversies, however, were settled to the liking of the media participant. Over the dissents of Justices Black and Douglas, the Supreme Court January 26, 1970 declined to review a $75,000 libel judgment won by Republican Senator Barry Goldwater of Arizona in a 1964 suit against Ralph Ginzburg, publisher of the magazine *Fact*; against Warren Boroson, *Fact*'s managing editor; and against the magazine itself (since defunct). The suit, filed when Goldwater was Republican candidate for President, cited an issue of *Fact* in which Goldwater was likeled to Adolf Hitler and was said to suffer from paranoia. Black argued that the court had failed to recognize that the Constitution protected a man's "unconditional right to print what he pleases about public affairs." He said reckless statements were "an inevitable and perhaps essential part of the process by which the public informs itself of the qualities of a man who would be President."

The Supreme Court May 18, 1970, however, unanimously overturned a $17,500 libel judgment that had been won by a Maryland developer against the *News Review*, a Greenbelt, Md. weekly newspaper. Bolstering the defense of the press against libel charges by public figures, the court held that the newspaper could not be penalized for performing a "wholly legitimate function" of accurately reporting that the developer, Charles S. Bresler, had been accused in public of "blackmail." In two former rulings, the court had restricted libel awards for public officials or public figures unless actual malice were demonstrated. The justices said the judge in Bresler's case had failed to instruct the jury accurately under libel rules laid down by the court. The opinion, written by Justice Potter Stewart, said it was "simply impossible to believe" that a reader could interpret the language reported in the news account as anything but "rhetorical hyperbole, a vigorous epithet used by those who considered Bresler's negotiating position extremely unreasonable." The press reports concerned city council debates on zoning restrictions that Bresler sought to have lifted. Justice Byron R. White concurred that the judge's instructions to the jury were in error but disagreed with the second part of Stewart's opinion. White said that "words of double meaning" like "blackmail" might be considered libelous in similar cases.

In three rulings handed down February 24, 1971, the Supreme Court reaffirmed its stand that the First Amendment protected the press against libel suits by public officials. The court said that unless malice were proved, the press could report charges of criminal behavior by politicians even though the charges were old, untrue or not related to the subject's public life.

In one of these three cases, the court voided a $20,000 award against the *Concord* (New Hampshire) *Monitor* and the North American Newspaper Alliance for a 1960 Drew Pearson column describing U.S. Senate candidate Alphonse Roy as a "former small-time bootlegger." The jury that awarded the judgment had held that the charge related to the private sector of Roy's life. Justice Stewart, writing for the court, said distinctions between public and private lives were "of little utility" for political candidates, "given the realities of our political life."

In the second case, the court reversed a $22,000 award to Mayor Leonard Damron of Crystal City, Fla., whoi had sued the *Ocala* (Florida) *Star-Banner* for publishing an incorrect story that the mayor had been charged with perjury. The perjury charges had been against the mayor's brother. The award had been upheld in lower courts on the ground that the charge did not relate to the mayor's official conduct, but the Supreme Court said that actual malice had not been proved and that the accusation was relevant.

In the third of the February 24 cases, over the dissent of Justice John M. Harlan, the court held that *Time* magazine was not guilty of malice in reporting charges of police brutality against Captain Frank Pape of Chicago without labeling the charges a "alleged." The charges had appeared in a 1961 report of the U.S. Civil Rights Commission, but the brutality had been alleged by a black homeowner, not by the commission.

The Supreme Court, in a 5-3 ruling June 7, 1971, broadened the protection of the press against libel suits brought by private individuals in cases of news accounts about matters of public interest. Justice Brennan, in the majority opinion, held that the same standards applied as laid down by the court for libel suits by public officials, that malice must be proved. Brennan wrote: "We honor the commitment to robust debate on public issues, which is embodied in the First Amendment, by extending constitutional protection to all discussion and communication involving matters of public and general concern, without regard to whether the persons involved are famous or anonymous." Joining in Brennan's opinion were Chief Justice Warren Earl Burger and Justice Harry A. Blackmun. Justices Black and White concurred in the result of Brennan's ruling but wrote separate opinions. Black restated his opinion, shared by Justice Douglas, that the Constitution prohibited all libel awards. White disagreed with Brennan's opinion to the extent that it would "shift the burden from those who publish to those who are injured," but he said the public had a right to know about official actions, such as the police arrest at issue in the case before the court.

Dissenting Justices Marshall and Stewart agreed that the press should have greater protection against libel suits by private persons, but they said the standard of libel should be negligence rather than malice. Although punitive damages should be eliminated, they argued, there should be awards for actual injury suffered. In a separate dissent, Justice Harlan said the press had a responsibility for exercising "reasonable care." Harlan also agreed that unrestrictd punitive damages should not be allowed.

The June 7 ruling overturned a $200,000 award won by George A. Rosenbloom, a Philadelphia magazine distributor, in a suit he had brought against Metromedia, Inc. The suit involved broadcasts on radio station WIP concerning Rosenbloom's arrest on charges of selling obscene literature. Bernard G. Segal, former president of the American Bar Association, represented Metromedia, and former Attorney General Ramsey Clark argued for Rosenbloom.

Three years later, however, the Supreme Court ruled, in a 5–4 decision June 25, 1974, that the press did not enjoy the same protection against libel suits filed by private persons that it did against suits by public figures. Private persons could recover "actual damages" for "defamatory falsehoods" without having to prove "actual malice," a condition required of public figures suing for libel. The holding reversed lower court decisions that overruled a $50,000 libel award to Chicago attorney Elmer Gertz. Gertz had been retained in 1969 by the parents of a youth who was fatally shot by a Chicago policeman in 1968. In March 1969, *American Opinion,* the monthly publication of the John Burch Society, printed an article that portrayed Gertz, who was then representing the parents in a civil suit against the policeman, as a "Communist-fronter" and as a participant in a "Communist campaign against the police."

Pointing out in his opinion for the court's majority that the article contained "serious inaccuracies" with references to Gertz, Justice Powell said that private persons should not have to prove as much as public officials. Public figures usually had access to the media to counteract false statements, and individuals seeking public prominence did so with the knowledge that they were inviting greater attention and the attendant risk of "defamatory falsehoods," Powell said. However, since the private person fit neither of the two public categories, he was more vulnerable to injury, and the "state interest in protecting . . . [him] is correspondingly greater."

Filing dissenting opinions were Chief Justice Burger and Justices Douglas, Brennan and White. In their dissent Douglas and Brennan argued that the decision would inhibit the press. Burger asserted that the court had offered a "new doctrinal theory which had no jurisprudential ancestry."

In a related decision, the court ruled June 26 that a labor union could not be sued for libel for publishing in its newsletter a list of "scabs"—men who did not cooperate with an organizing drive. The union had also printed a definition of a "scab" attributed to the American writer Jack London, who had called a scab a "traitor to his God, country, his family and his class." "Uninhibited, robust and wide-open debate" in a labor dispute need not result in a libel action, the court held. Dissenting were Chief Justice Burger and Justices William H. Rehnquist and Powell.

In a further situation involving libel suits by public figures, the Supreme Court, in two 8-1 decisions June 26, 1979, narrowed the definition of "public figure." This action, taken in two cases, made it easier for individuals who had unwillingly appeared in a public light—and therefore were not voluntary public figures—to sue for libel. A public figure had to prove actual malice whereas a non-public figure could win a case by proving negligence. The rulings came in separate cases, *Hutchinson* v. *Proxmire* and *Wolston* v. *Reader's Digest Association, Inc.*

Hutchinson v. *Proxmire* involved a libel suit brought against Democratic Senator William Proxmire of Wisconsin by a scientist, Ronald R. Hutchinson. In a 1976 newsletter, Proxmire had ridiculed a government-funder research project headed by Hutchinson. The Senator made Hutchinson a "winner" of his monthly "Golden Fleece" award, a derisive prize for agencies and persons who, in Proxmire's opinion, wasted federal money. Hutchinson's suit had been summarily dismissed by the U.S. Seventh Circuit Court of Appeals on two grounds: (1) that the "speech of debate" clause of the Constitution immunized Proxmire from lawsuits, and (2) that Hutchinson was a public figure because he had received grants from the government for his scientific research.

The Supreme Court reversed the appeals court decision and held that the suit against Proxmire could be tried in lower federal courts. The high court, led by Chief Justice Burger, found that the "speech or debate" clause did not shield members of Congress from the consequences of performing such actions as publishing newsletters or publicly criticizing others through personal "awards." Justice Brennan, arguing for a broad interpretation of the clause, dissented in this aspect of the case. Burger said that despite the scientist's use of public grants, Hutchinson had "not thrust himself or his views into public controversy to influence others."

In the second case, *Wolston v. Reader's Digest Association, Inc.*, a Russian translator named Ilya Wolston had sued *Reader's Digest* because the magazine in 1974 had published a book placing him on a list of alleged Soviet agents who had been "convicted of espionage or falsifying information or perjury and/or contempt charges following espionage indictments. The Russian-born plaintiff had never been indicted for or convicted of espionage, although he had been subpoenaed by a grand jury investigating the activities of a member of his family who later pleaded guilty to spy charges. (He was a nephew of the confessed Soviet spies Myra and Jack Soble.) Wolston had failed to answer the subpoena and was cited for criminal contempt of court in 1958. He was then given a one-year suspended sentence and put on probation for three years. Lower federal courts, ruling that Wolston was a public figure, had thrown out his suit against *Reader's Digest*.

The Supreme Court reversed the dismissal and unanimously ruled that Wolston's suit could proceed. All nine justices agreed that Wolston deserved to have his suit tried, but Justice Brennan alone contended that Wolston had enough evidence of "actual malice" to warrant a trial. Justices Blackmun and Marshall maintained that Wolston was not a public figure in 1979, even if he had been one in 1958. Justice Rehnquist stated that Wolston's citation for criminal contempt was not enough to qualify him as a public figure. He rejected "the further contention that any person who engages in criminal conduct automatically becomes a public figure for purposes of comment on a limited range of issues relating to his conviction." "To hold otherwise," Rehnquist warned, "would create an 'open season' for all who sought to defame persons convicted of crime.

Journalists' Thoughts Not Protected

Outspoken fears of thought police and of the Orwellian "Big Brother" were provoked by a media case settled in 1979. In a 6-3 decision April 18, the Supreme Court ruled that journalists could not rely on the First Amendment to avoid answering questions about their "state of mind" when they became the targets of libel suits by public figures. The decision, in *Herbert* v. *Lando,* reversed a November 7, 1977 ruling of a three-judge panel of the U.S. Second Circuit Court of Appeals.

The case involved Anthony B. Herbert, a former lieutenant colonel in the Army, who left the service after accusing his superiors of covering up Vietnam atrocities. Herbert's allegations received considerable publicity in the early 1970s. The CBS television news program "60 Minutes" February 4, 1973 broadcast an episode entitled "The Selling of Colonel Herbert." The program cast doubt on Herbert's charges. Herbert subsequently filed a $44-million libel suit against the network—naming as co-defendants "60 Minutes" producer Barry Lando and correspondent Mike Wallace—and *The Atlantic Monthly* magazine, which had published an article on the program. He charged that the show had "deliberately distorted the record through selective investigation, 'skillful' editing and one-sided interviewing."

Herbert's suit became stalled in the pretrial stage because Lando refused to answer a number of questions asked by the plaintiff's lawyer. The questions related to the producer's thoughts and intentions while putting together the "60 Minutes" episode. A federal district court ordered Lando to answer the questions. The order was overturned by the appeals court. In an opinion written by Chief Judge Irving R. Kaufman of the appeals court, the panel held that the questions struck at the "heart of the vital human component of the editorial process. . . . Faced with the possibility of such an inquisition, reporters and journalists would be reluctant to express their doubts. Indeed, they would be chilled in the very process of thought." Kaufman called unrestricted judicial inquiry into journalistic thought processes an "invasion of First Amendment rights." Judge James L. Oakes concurred in this opinion. Judge Thomas J. Meskill dissented, arguing that the "major purpose" of the lawsuit was "to expose the defendants' subjective state of mind . . . to the light of judicial review. . . . The publication of lies should be discouraged."

The Supreme Court reversed the appeals court holding. The high court based its reversal on an interpretation of the 1964 ruling in *New York Times* v. *Sullivan,* which had established the legal precedent that in order for a public figure to collect damages for libel, he had to show that the defendant had acted with "actual malice."

Writing for the majority in the Herbert case, Justice Byron R.

White held that the *New York Times* decision "made it essential to proving liability that plaintiffs focus on the conduct and state of mind of the defendant. . . . Inevitably, unless liability is to be completely foreclosed, the thoughts and editorial processes of the alleged defamer would be open to examination." Rejecting the press' argument that a finding for Herbert would lead to increased "self-censorship" by the media, White wrote that "if the claimed inhibition flows from the fear of damages liability for publishing knowing or reckless statements, those effects are precisely what [the 1964 case] and other cases have held to be consistent with the First Amendment. Spreading false information in and of itself carries no First Amendment credentials."

Justice Lewis F. Powell, Jr. issued an opinion concurring with White but warning that courts must strike "a proper balance" between First Amendment interests and private interests in libel cases. Justices Potter Stewart, William J. Brennan, Jr. and Thurgood Marshall each dissented separately. Each said he found that the appeals court had extended too broad a protection for journalists in libel suits. Stewart asserted that the effect of the *New York Times* case was to rule out inquiries into the "editorial process." The key in libel cases, he declared, was the material a journalist published, not "his motivation in publishing it." Brennan said he would allow questions about an individual journalist's "state of mind" but would shield from inquiry newsroom conversations unless the plaintiff could show that "the libel in question constitutes defamatory falsehood." Marshall, too, said he would permit defendants to be questioned about their "state of mind" but only under the careful supervision of a trial judge. The "substance of editorial conversation," he held, should not be part of the inquiry.

Many newspapers and other elements of the news media angrily attacked the *Herbert* decision. Several media spokesmen linked the ruling to other recent instances of what they considered to be attacks on the press by the nation's courts. William A. Leonard, president of CBS News, said April 18 that the ruling was "another invasion into the nation's newsrooms." The decision, he charged, denied "constitutional protection to the journalist's most precious possessions—his mind, his thoughts and his editorial judgment."

Jack C. Landau, director of the Reporters Committee for Freedom of the Press, said April 18 that the Supreme Court seemed "to consider any societal interest more important than the First Amendment." He warned that "the press will soon have lost the last constitutional shred of its editorial privacy and independence from the government."

The Newark *Star-Ledger* April 20 denounced the decision as "an Orwellian ruling" and "another grave blow" to freedom of the press. "The court does not appear to be concerned with press responsibility for objectivity," the *Star-Ledger* charged; "it now wants an accounting of what's going on in a newsman's mind when he or she is writing a story."

Allen H. Neuharth, chairman of Gannett Company and president of the American Newspaper Publishers Association (ANPA), said at the annual ANPA convention in New York April 23 that the high court had "battered holes in the First Amendment big enough to drive the Constitution through. . . . The courts have destroyed our shield laws, sent our reporters to jail, held our editors in contempt and fined publishers." Neuharth said that the "Burger Court" in particular, and the judiciary in general, were "developing a state of mind that it is above the law, even above the Constitution." (The ANPA announced April 23 that is was establishing a "First Amendment legal fund," financed by the richer newspapers, to aid smaller newspapers in fights over press freedom.)

Tom Wicker had charged in his *New York Times* column April 20 that the court "has undoubtedly 'chilled' the willingness of the press to go after and make public controversial material that might result in an expensive and time-consuming libel suit." He conceded that "on occasion, this may well prevent an inaccurate or misleading story from appearing." He held, however, that "far more often, it is likely to mean the public will be deprived of legitimate and important information believed to be accurate but perhaps not provably so in court—or not without expense and effort that a newspaper or broadcaster cannot afford."

The *Des Moines Register* warned editorially April 22 that "grilling of journalists about their thoughts, opinions and conclusions belongs in a police state, not a free society."

Although most press comment on the *Herbert* decision was critical, often vehemently so, not all press representatives appeared to be very distressed by the ruling.

The Salt Lake Tribune of Salt Lake City noted editorially April 21 that "the reactions from journalists . . . can be most generally condensed as 'a major defeat for the First Amendment' and worry that the decision will have a 'chilling effect' on press freedoms and the right of the public to receive information vital to the conduct of public affairs." But "we don't wholly endorse" these views, the *Tribune* asserted. "Of course, there are dangers that the decision will inhibit the press' ambitions to inquire into matters of public concern. However, these dangers aren't as great as the general reaction of abhorrence suggests. Justice White reminds us that the federal laws require that the deposition-discovery process 'be construed to secure the just, speedy, and inexpensive determination of every action.' He further admonishes, 'District courts should not neglect their power to restrict discovery where "justice requires [protection] for a party or person from annoyance, embarrassment, oppression, or undue burden or expense." ' Also, Justice White tell the lower courts, 'With this authority at hand, judges should not hesitate to exercise appropriate control over the discovery process.' What the Supreme court has effectively said is that while inquiry to determine 'actual malice' can be made into the 'state of mind' of editors and reporters . . . that inquiry can . . . be restricted to reasonable lengths and depths and that district judges have an obligation to set appropriate limits.

In an April 22 editorial, *Newsday* (Garden City, N.Y.) agreed that "neither press nor public need panic for now. Responsible journalists have always striven to report the news without favor or malice, to the extent that human frailty permits. And we do not find it easy to conceive of a situation where a genuinely responsible journalist would be prejudiced by explaining the standards of his decisionmaking to an equally responsible court. . . ."

The *Minneapolis Tribune* pointed out April 24 that in the *Herbert* ruling, the court had not restricted press freedom but had merely refused to extend it. "Defendants in libel cases have routinely answered questions about their motives and judgments," the *Tribune* asserted, "and the court simply maintained the *status quo*. Thus it is both inappropriate and misleading to claim that the ruling constitutes a new threat to journalists' ability to do their jobs."

The following month Justice Marshall publicly criticized his fellow Supreme Court justices May 27 for affording "insufficient protection to constitutional rights" in a pair of 1979 cases. Mar-

Libel Laws as Media Curbs

shall's remarks, make in a speech at the annual meeting of the Second Judicial Circuit in Buck Hill Falls, Pa., alluded to the *Herbert* ruling and to the court's decision in *Bell* v. *Wolfish*. (In the latter case, the court had ruled that pretrial detainees were subject to strict jail procedures.) Of the *Herbert* ruling, Marshall said that "preserving a climate of free interchange among journalists is essential to sound editorial decision-making."

Bruce W. Sanford, an attorney practicing communications law for various news organizations, reported in the September-October 1979 issue of the *Columbia Journalism Review* that "most news-media lawyers" consider the *Herbert* ruling to be of "minor legal significance." They regarded it, he wrote, as "a sensible, unsurprising decision which hardly changes libel law at all, other than to put it back where it was before Judge Irving Kaufman . . . fashioned . . . a dazzling new privilege to safeguard the editorial process." Even reporters, he wrote finally concluded that the decision did them little or no harm. *Washington Post* reporter Tom Reid was quoted as saying that he and his *Post* colleagues "agreed that we'd never end up testifying that we doubted the truth of a story."

Justice Brennan, although he had dissented in part in the *Herbert* decision, asserted October 17, 1979 that the press had "overreacted" in its attack on the ruling. He noted that the *New York Times* v. *Sullivan* ruling of 1964 and the *Gertz* v. *Robert Welch, Inc.* ruling of 1974, taken together, provided (a) that to sue a media defendant successfully for libel, a public figure had to prove that defamatory material was issued with "actual malice," and (b) that actual malice "turned on the media defendant's 'subjective awareness of probable falsity.'" The *Sullivan* principle, Brennan said, "was that if the media were liable for large damage judgments for the publication of false defamatory information, the resulting inhibitions might undermine the robust public discussion so essential to a democracy. If a journalist knew that he was publishing defamatory falsehood, however, the First Amendment would offer him no protection."

Brennan held that it was "clear that a journalist's state of mind is relevant to his 'subjective awareness of probable falsity,' and thus to the issue of actual malice." Traditionally, he said, "a plaintiff is entitled to discovery on all relevant issues. Privileges are rare and strictly construed. Nevertheless, the press argued that it could not perform its functions under the First Amendment unless special 'editorial' privilege were created to shield it from such inquiries." The Supreme Court's rejection of the press' argument evoked "a virtually unprecedented outpouring of scathing criticism," Brennan declared. He noted that the managing editor of the *St. Louis Post-Dispatch* had denounced the opinion as having "the potential of totally inhibiting the press to a degree seldom seen outside a dictatorial or fascist country."

The decision "deserved a more considered response from the press that it received," Brennan declared. "The injury done the press was simply not of the magnitude to justify the resulting firestorm or acrimonious criticism. In its rush to cudgel the court, the press acted as if the decision imposed restrictions on what the press could say. . . . In fact, two newspapers [the New Orleans *Times-Picayune* April 20 and the Birmingham News April 19] erroneously characterized the opinion as holding that truth would no longer be an absolute defense to libel suits." Other press comments were similarly "examples of inaccurate reporting," Brennan said.

The "deepest source of the press' outrage," Brennan observed, "was I think well captured" by CBS News President William Leonard's complaint that the decision deprived journalists of constitutional protection of their "most precious possessions"—their minds, thoughts and editorial judgment. "I understand and sympathize with Mr. Leonard's concern," Brennan said. ". . . Nevertheless, the inquiry into a defendant's state of mind, into his intent, is one of the most common procedures in the law. Almost all crimes require that some element of the defendant's intent be established, as do all intentional torts, such as trespass, assault or conversion. . . . And, in the area of libel, it would scarcely be fair to say that a plaintiff can only recover if he establishes intentional falsehood and at the same time to say that he cannot inquire into a defendant's intentions."

Carol Burnett Wins Suit Against National Enquirer

The actress Carol Burnett, after a five-year struggle, won a highly publicized libel suit against the Florida-based *National Enquirer*. A Los Angeles Superior Court jury concluded March 27, 1981 that the defendant publication had libeled the actress in a brief article in March 1976, and it awarded her $1.6 million in damages (a sum that later was halved). The eleven-member jury unanimously agreed that the *Enquirer* should pay Miss Burnett $300,000 in general damages and $1.3 million in punitive damages. It acted on its finding that the weekly tabloid had knowingly printed false, defamatory information about the comedienne.

The suit was based on a March 2, 1976 article in which the *Enquirer* said: "At a Washington restaurant, a boisterous Carol Burnett had a loud argument with another diner, [then Secretary of State] Henry Kissinger. She traipsed around the place offering everyone a bite of her dessert. But Carol really raised eyebrows when she accidently knocked a glass of wine over one diner and started giggling instead of apologizing. The guy wasn't amused and 'accidently' spilled a glass of water over Carol's dress."

The *Enquirer*, under pressure, later printed a retraction, and acknowledged that the article was inaccurate. Miss Burnett rejected the retraction. The key issue in the case was whether the *Enquirer* had published the article with "actual malice"—with knowledge that it was false or in reckless disregard for the truth.

During the seven-day trial, Miss Burnett denounced the article as a "disgusting pack of lies." Testifying that both of her parents had died of the effects of alcoholism, she said that depicting her as "drunk" had caused her to lose credibility in her campaign against alcoholism. Eighteen witnesses for the actress, two of them employees of the restaurant, the Rive Gauche in Georgetown, testified that the *Enquirer* article was inaccurate. Kissinger also denied its accuracy.

The *Enquirer* did not defend the truth of its article. It based much of its defense on what its attorney, William A. Masterson, called "the First Amendment issue." The defense said that the information on which the article was based had come from an informant considered reliable. Staff members had acted responsibly in trying to confirm its accuracy, the defense claimed. The writer whose byline appeared over the article, however, asserted in a deposition that he had not trusted the source and that the article actually had been written by an *Enquirer* senior editor. Another reporter testified that he had been asked to check the article for accuracy about an hour before deadline. Although he was unable to do so sufficiently, he said, a senior editor had pressured him to approve the article.

The verdict was lauded jubilantly by many show-business and other celebrities who had accused the *Enquirer* of printing false, defamatory articles about them. Even the press largely supported the verdict, suggesting in some cases that the publication's bad reputation as much as the facts of the case was the motivation for approving attacks on the *Enquirer*.

The Lincoln (Nebraska) *Star*, which described the judgment as "simple justice," asserted editorially March 28 that "the *Enquirer* seeks to sell copies by purveying titillating, sordid, juicy items about figures in the public eye. It preys largely on uninformed people seeking psychological relief from humdrum lives. . . . The libel judgment should have had no effect on responsibility—even though controversial—reporting and commentary. It will not make it more dangerous to tell the truth."

The Hartford (Connecticut) *Courant* asserted March 29 that the *Enquirer* "loves to purvey sleazy news about celebrities" and that it "got its just desserts." While "its invocation of the First Amendment in its defense is both obnoxious and self-serving," the *Courant* declared, "the defense has some relevance and may ultimately win the day on appeal. Free press rights, like free speech and free assembly rights, are not confined to those in our society who behave 'responsibly.' They apply also to the extremes, however much they are disdained by most of the public."

The Louisville (Kentucky) *Courier-Journal* agreed March 29 that the *Enquirer* "doubtless got what it deserved." The *Courier-Journal* said "few reputable journalists will shed tears that a purveyor of titillating garbage has suddenly been forced to recognize that the rights of the press carry responsibilities, too."

The *Sentinel Star* of Orlando, Fla. suggested March 28 that "while we should not understate a concern that such decisions might unnecessarily restrict legitimate reporting efforts or encourage frivolous lawsuits by public figures . . . , the media might still benefit from the verdict. Every newspaper, magazine, radio and television operation makes mistakes and will continue to do so. Too often, though, all the media are painted by the same brush that colors the *National Enquirer* as irresponsible. The Burnett jury has helped note that there is a distinction. . . ."

Free Press Versus Fair Trial

Rights in Conflict

Rights sometimes are in competition—or in conflict. On occasion, the First Amendment's guarantee of a free press has appeared to conflict with the Sixth Amendment's competing provision that "in all criminal prosecutions, the accused shall enjoy the right to a speedy and public trial, by an impartial jury of the state and district wherein the crime shall have been committed . . . [and] to have compulsory process for obtaining witnesses in his favor. . . ." The dilemma was pointed up by the late Supreme Court Justice Hugo L. Black in 1941 when he noted that "free speech and fair trials are two of the most cherished policies of our civilization, and it would be a trying task to choose between them."

"The problems arise," reported then-Assistant Attorney General Richard L. Thornburgh May 28, 1976 at the judicial conference of the District of Columbia Circuit, "where the actions of a completely free press may prevent a fair trial. Which are we to choose? The Supreme Court has said that the most fundamental of all freedoms is a fair trial. But James Madison thought that his proposed amendment to the Constitution relating to free speech, press and conscience was the most valuable amendment of the nine which he submitted."

The "free press-fair trial controversy" was investigated in 1976 by the staff of the Senate Constitutional Rights Subcommittee. In a preface to the staff report, Subcommittee Chairman John V. Tunney, then a Democratic Senator from California, asserted that "while a democratic society must continually weigh the right of the individual against the societal interest, it is the Subcommittee's view that in the occasional collision between free press and fair trial, neither of these 'cherished policies' need yield to the other." "In recent years," he wrote, "with the rise of modern communications and news-gathering techniques, information concerning a trial is much more readily and broadly disseminated, often on a national scale. While this broad dissemination can serve to preserve the integrity of the judicial proceeding, it may, on occasion work against the defendant. The right to an impartial jury, for example, may not be served by extensive pretrial publicity. . . ."

The staff report elaborated to some extent: "The advantages of free press coverage of criminal trials are many. The defendant is protected from intimidation by the prosecution. Society is exposed to the workings of the criminal justice system. Those who would commit similar crimes may be deterred by observing that some get caught. And, those who would change the system can collect examples of specific instances where the laws or the courts or the legal profession have failed. There are also some disadvantages of unfettered press coverage of criminal trials—primarily the prejudicial effect such publicity may have on a defendant's right to a fair trial. For, like other institutions, the press is capable of error. There are occasions when the reporting of a criminal trial is excessive, inaccurate, unfair, or indiscreet. . . ."

Pretiral Publicity & Sheppard Verdict

The potential for a clash between free-press and fair-trial rights was illustrated by the case of Dr. Samuel H. Sheppard. A result of the Sheppard case—and of the Supreme Court decision assailing the publicity surrounding it—was a spate of "gag orders" issued by judges to keep "prejudicial" news reports from tainting the impartiality of juries.

Sheppard, then 30, a socially prominent osteopathic surgeon of Bay Village, Ohio, had been convicted in Cleveland December 21, 1954 of second-degree murder in the death of his pregnant wife,

Marilyn, 31. Common Pleas Judge Edward Blythin imposed the mandatory sentence of life imprisonment.

The staff report of the Senate Constitutional Rights Subcommittee found that "the following conditions prevailed" in the Sheppard case: "Throughout the entire pretrial period virulent and incriminating publicity about the defendant and the murder of his wife made the case notorious. The news media frequently aired charges and countercharges in addition to those for which the defendant was tried. Three months before trial, the defendant was examined for more than five hours without counsel in a televised three-day inquest conducted before an audience of several hundred spectators in a gymnasium. Over three weeks before the trial the newspapers published the names and addresses of prospective jurors causing them to receive letters and telephone calls about the case. Newsmen were allowed to take over almost the entire small courtroom, harassing the defendant, and most of the trial participants. Twenty reporters were assigned seats by the court within the bar and in close proximity to the jury and counsel, precluding privacy between the defendant and his counsel. A broadcasting station was assigned space next to the jury room. Pervasive publicity was given to the case throughout the trial, most of it involving incriminating evidence not introduced at the trial. At least some of this highly prejudicial publicity reached the jurors. From the day of Mrs. Sheppard's murder, some of the more striking newspaper headlines dealt with: (1) Sheppard's refusal to take a lie detector test; (2) scientific blood tests (never presented as evidence at trial) refuting Sheppard's version of events; (3) Sheppard's general uncooperativeness with police authorities; (4) Sheppard's extramarital love affairs as a motive for the crime."

The Sheppard conviction was reversed by an 8-1 Supreme Court decision June 6, 1966 on the ground that "the state trial judge did not fulfill his duty to protect Sheppard from the inherently prejudicial publicity which saturated the community and to control disruptive influences in the courtroom." Justice Hugo L. Black was the sole dissenter.

Sheppard had been released in 1964 under a writ of *habeas corpus* after Federal District Court Judge Carl A. Weinman July 15 ordered him freed on bail. Weinman described the trial as a "mockery of justice." The writ was canceled by the Sixth Circuit Court of Appeals, but Sheppard remained free on bail pending the Supreme Court appeal. The Supreme Court decision reversed the denial of *habeas corpus* and ordered the case against Sheppard dropped "unless the state puts him to its charges again within a reasonable time." (Sheppard was acquitted November 16 after a second trial.)

Justice Tom C. Clark, author of the Supreme Court's majority opinion, cited "the massive pretrial publicity" and "the carnival atmosphere at the trial." He criticized the trial judge for failing to take steps "to reduce the appearance of prejudicial material and to protect the jury from outside influence." The trial court, he said, should have "more closely regulated the conduct of newsmen in the courtroom," should have "insulated the witnesses" and should "have made some effort to control the release of leads, information, and gossip to the press by police officers, witnesses, and the counsel for both sides."

Clark said that the Supreme Court had "consistently required that the press have a free hand" and had "been unwilling to place any direct limitations on the freedom traditionally exercised by the news media." But, he insisted, "the courts must take such steps by rule and regulation what will protect their processes from prejudicial outside interferences. . . . Collaboration between counsel and the press as to information affecting the fairness of a criminal trial is not only subject to regulation but is highly censurable and worthy of disciplinary measures." "Given the pervasiveness of modern communications and the difficulty of effacing prejudicial publicity from the minds of the jurors," Clark declared, "the trial courts must take strong measures to ensure that the balance is never weighed against them."

Publicity & Calley's Vietnam Atrocity Trial

The case of First Lieutenant William L. Calley, Jr., convicted by an Army court-martial March 29, 1971 in a highly publicized Vietnam atrocity trial, also became embroiled in the conflict between the rights of free press and of fair trial.

The military jury found Calley guilty of the premeditated murder of at least twenty-two South Veitnamese civilians who had died at Mylai March 16, 1968, and the tribunal sentenced Calley to life imprisonment. The case, during the height of the emotional controversy over American conduct in Vietnam, was covered intensively by the media and became an international *cause celebre*.

The Army Court of Review February 16, 1973 upheld Calley's conviction and sentence. The review panel rejected various grounds for reversal, among them the contention that the verdict was influenced by pretrial publicity.

The conviction was overturned, however, by U.S. District Court Judge J. Robert Elliott in Columbus, Georgia September 25, 1974 on the ground that "massive adverse pretrial publicity" had made a fair trial under military law an impossibility. "Never in the history of the military justice system, and perhaps in the history of American courts," said Elliott, "has an accused ever encountered such intense and continuous prejudicial publicity." The judge cited the use of such words and phrases as "atrocity," "slaughter of noncombatants," "barbaric act" and similar descriptions in the media coverage of Mylai. He was especially critical of the reporting of eyewitness accounts of the incident. He rebuked one of the television networks for using bloody splotches on a map of Vietnam to locate the site of the killings. This, he said, was "blood-horror visual technique." Elliott cited other grounds for reversal as well.

Elliott's decision was then overturned by the U.S. Fifth Circuit Court of Appeals in New Orleans September 10, 1975. The appellate panel, reinstating Calley's conviction, rejected Elliott's contention that the media had made a fair trial impossible. According to the appellate court, the harm of the publicity had been offset by the military court's scrupulous care in picking a jury and providing other safeguards. The Supreme Court declined April 5, 1976 to review the conviction. (Calley, whose sentence had been reduced, had been free on bail since November 9, 1974. The Army said April 5, 1976 that Calley would remain free but under some parole restrictions.)

Barring the Press from the Courtroom

Courts have occasionally tried to assure fair trials by barring the media from the courtroom. The judicial pronouncements that resulted have not clarified the media's rights to everybody's satisfaction.

Wide controversy over the closing of a courtroom resulted from the state court proceedings against Carmine Persico in New York City in 1971. Persico, charged with conspiracy and extortion, went on trial November 8. After the trial began, *The New York*

Times, the *New York Daily News* and the *New York Post* printed articles linking Persico with organized crime, revealing that he was nicknamed "Carmine the Snake" and discussing his criminal record. The defense counsel moved for the mistrial on the ground that such prejudicial reports diminished Persico's chances of getting a fair trial. The judge polled the jury and found that none of the jurors had read the articles. He therefore rejected the mistrial motion. But the judge denounced the articles as unfair and hinted that he might consider contempt charges against any newsman whose stories on the trial exceeded the information revealed in the courtroom.

All three newspapers then published material both reporting on the judge's warning and summarizing the articles that had invoked the warning. Defense counsel thereupon again moved for a mistrial or, alternatively, for the closing of the courtroom to public and press. The attorney waived his client's "First Amendment rights to a public trial in order to insure his Sixth Amendment's [sic] right to a fair trial." Over the prosecution's objection, the judge granted the alternative request and closed the courtroom.

A group of journalists sued, requesting that the trial judge be ordered to reopen the proceedings. The request was denied by an appellate panel, which ruled that it was the defendant rather than the public or the press to whom a public trial was guaranteed. The precedent cited was a 1954 appellate decision arising out of a trial (*People* v. *Jelke*) on compulsory prostitution charges. In the 1954 case, the judge had cited "the interests of good morals" in closing the courtroom over the objection of the defendant. The appellate panel decided that the defendant's Sixth Amendment right to a public trial had been violated. A petition by journalists (*Matter of United Press Assns.* v. *Valente*) against the 1954 courtroom closing was dismissed as moot, however, with the Court of Appeals, New York State's highest court, asserting that the journalists sought "to convert what is essentially the right of the particular accused into a privilege for every citizen, a privilege which the latter may invoke independently of, and even in hostility to, the rights of the accused." Such a privilege "cannot be," according to the 1954 decision, "for it would deprive an accused of all power to waive his right to a public trial and thereby prevent him from taking a course which he may believe best for his own interests."

Persico was acquitted before the Court of Appeals could rule on the appeal of the journalists against the rejection of their petition. The Court of Appeals heard the journalists' appeal January 3, 1972, and it ruled March 22 that the trial judge had been wrong to close the courtroom. The Court of Appeals found it unnecessary to consider the Sixth Amendment issue. It held that the judge had acted to punish the press rather than to defend the defendant's right to a fair trial. The precedent of *United Press Assns.*, therefore, did not apply, the judges ruled. According to the Court of Appeals, the closing of a courtroom to the media could be justified only by a showing that "it was necessary to meet 'a serious and imminent threat' to 'the integrity of the trial.' . . ."

A report on closed trials was adopted by the Committee on Civil Rights of the Association of the Bar of the City of New York. The report, published in the official *Record* of the association in November 1972, conceded that "whenever an individual is charged with a crime which receives substantial news coverage, there arises the potential for collision between the right to an impartial trial . . . and the right to a free press. . . ." "While some limitations upon the press have been required, permitted, or cited approvingly in order to protect the right to an impartial trial," the report said, "we can find neither precedent nor justification for so sweeping a curtailment of so basic a constitutional right as is inherent in closing a trial or placing publication restrictions upon the press."

A different aspect of the courtroom-closing issue received an airing in 1979. The Supreme Court July 2 ruled, 5-4, that the public and press enjoyed no right under the Sixth Amendment to attend pretrial criminal hearings. The ruling, in the case of *Gannett Co. v. DePasquale,* gave trial judges broad discretion in closing their courtrooms if they feared that the due process rights of the accused would be jeopardized by publicity. Although the decision involved pretrial hearings (on whether there were grounds to suppress specific evidence from trial), some legal experts concluded that it could be applied by trial judges to exclude the public and press from full-scale criminal trials.

The ruling concerned a November 4, 1976 hearing on the admissibility of evidence in a case involving the disappearance and apparent murder of a former policeman in Henrietta, N.Y. The trial judge, Daniel A. DePasquale, acting on a request of the defense counsel, and with the agreement of the prosecution, had closed the courtroom to the press. The Gannett Co. had challenged the judge's action. The New York State Court of Appeals upheld the judge's action.

The Supreme court, affirming the state court judgment, held that neither the Sixth Amendment nor the Fourteenth Amendment guaranteed the public access to pretrial criminal proceedings. Nor could the First Amendment be invoked by the press to gain entrance to such hearings, the court said.

Writing for the majority, Justice Potter Stewart held that "the Constitution nowhere mentions any right of access to a criminal trial on the part of the public; its guarantee, like the others enumerated, is personal to the accused." He maintained that "to safeguard the due process rights of the accused, a trial judge has an affirmative constitutional duty to minimize the effects of prejudicial pretrial publicity. And because of the Constitution's pervasive concern for these due process rights a trial judge may surely take protective measures even when they are not strictly and inescapably necessary. Publicity concerning pretrial suppression hearings . . . poses special risks of unfairness. The whole purpose of such hearings is to screen out unreliable or illegally obtained evidence and insure that this evidence does not become known to the jury. Publicity concerning the proceedings at a pretrial hearing . . . could influence public opinion against a defendant and inform potential jurors of inculpatory information wholly inadmissable at the actual trial. . . . Closure of pretrial proceedings is often one of the most effective methods that a trial judge can emply to attempt to insure that the fairness of a trial will not be jeopardized by the dissemination of such information . . . before the trial itself has even begun." Stewart pointed out, furthermore, that "any denial of access in this case was not absolute but only temporary. Once the danger of prejudice had dissipated, a transcript of the suppression hearing was made available. . . . [T]he press . . . had the opportunity to inform the public of the details of the pretrial hearing accurately and completely. . . ."

Stewart's opinion was endorsed by Justices John Paul Stevens, William J. Rehnquist and Lewis F. Powell, Jr. and by Chief Justice Warren E. Burger. Burger emphasized the difference between pretrial hearings and trials and suggested that restrictions that were constitutional for pretrial proceedings might not be constitutional at actual trials. Powell said that Judge DePasquale had considered the media's First Amendment rights before closing the courtroom. He recalled that the Supreme court had previously "stressed" (in *Estes* v. *Texas*) that "the presence of the press at judicial proceedings must be limited when it is apparent that the accused might otherwise be prejudiced or disadvantaged." "The right of access to courtroom proceedings, of course, is not absolute," he wrote. "It is limited both by the constitutional right of defendants to a fair trial and by the needs of government to obtain just convictions and to preserve the confidentiality of sensitive information and the identity of informants. The task of determining the application of these limitations . . . falls almost exclusively upon the trial court asked to exclude members of the press and public from the courtroom." Powell stressed the importance of the requirement that the Supreme Court "identify for the guidance of trial courts the constitutional standards by which they are to judge whether closure is justified, and the minimal procedure by which this procedure is to be applied."

In his concurring opinion, Rehnquist wrote that the Supreme Court "today holds" that "the Sixth Amendment does not require a criminal trial or hearing to be opened to the public if the participants to the litigation agree for any reason . . . that it should be closed." The Supreme Court "repeatedly has held that there is no First Amendment right of access in the public or the press to judicial or other proceedings," he continued. Rehnquist asserted that the court had "emphatically" rejected the proposition in Powell's concurring opinion "that the First Amendment is some sort of constitutional 'sunshine law' that requires notice, an opportunity to be heard and substantial reasons before a governmental proceeding may be closed to the public and press." Rehnquist held that lower courts "remain, in the best tradition of our federal system, free to determine for themselves the question whether to open or close the proceeding."

Justices Harry A. Blackmun, William J. Brennan, Jr., Byron R. White and Thurgood Marshall dissented. "Today's decision, as I see it, is an unfortunate one," wrote Blackmun in his minority opinion. ". . . The result is that the important interests of the public and the press . . . in open judicial proceedings are rejected and cast aside as of little value or significance." The Sixth Amendment "reflects the tradition of our system of criminal justice that a trial is a 'public event' and that '[w]hat transpires in the courtroom is public property," Blackmun held. He conceded that "[b]y its literal terms the Sixth Amendment secures the right to a public trial only to 'the accused' And in this case the accused were the ones who sought to waive that right, and to have the public removed . . . in order to guard against publicity that possibly would be prejudicial to them."

Blackmun pointed out, however, that the Supreme Court had "previously . . . recognized that the Sixth Amendment may implicate interests beyond those of the accused." Previous rulings, he asserted, made it clear "that the fact the Sixth Amendment casts the right to a public trial in terms of the right of the accused is not sufficient to permit the inferrence that the accused may compel a private proceeding simply by waiving that right." He cited the history of the open trial to indicate that the ban on closed trials served such public purposes as checking judicial abuse and partiality—a partiality that might favor the accused as easily as it might harm him. Blackmun said he had found "no evidence in the development of the public trial concept . . . and in the adoption of the Sixth Amendment to indicate . . . a right to a private proceeding or a power to compel a private trial arising out of the ability to waive the grant of a public one." He refused to "indulge in a mere mechanical inference that, by phrasing the public trial as one belonging to the accused, the framers of the Amendment must have meant the accused to have the power to dispense with publicity."

Blackmun reported that he also found "good reason to hold" that the Sixth Amendment's public-trial provision applies to suppression hearings held apart from the trial. Such a hearing, he asserted, "resembles and relates to the full trial in almost every particular. . . . Moreover, the pretrial suppression hearing often is critical, and it may be decisive. . . ." The hearing may make the trial itself unnecessary, and it "often is the only judicial proceeding of substantial importance that takes place during a criminal prosecution," he noted. He concluded that "a pretrial suppression hearing is the close equivalent of the trial on the merits for purposes of applying the public trial provisions of the Sixth Amendment," and he held that "for purposes of the Sixth Amendment public trial provision the pretrial suppression hearing at issue in this case must be considered part of the trial."

"I do not deny that the publication of information learned in an open proceeding may harm irreparably, under certain circumstances, the ability of a defendant to obtain a fair trial," Blackmun wrote. ". . . Although the Sixth Amendment's public trial provision establishes a strong presumption in favor of open proceedings, it does not require that all proceedings be held in open court when to do so would deprive a defendant of a fair trial. . . . [Courts] have recognized exceptions to the public trial requirement even when it is the accused who objects to the exclusion of the public or a portion thereof. . . . [The Sixth Amendment] does not prevent a trial court from restricting access to a pretrial suppression hearing where such restriction is necessary in order to ensure that a defendant not be denied a fair trial as a result of prejudicial publicity flowing from that hearing. At the same time, however, the public's interest in maintaining open courts requires that any exception to the rule be narrowly drawn. . . ."

Media spokesmen denounced the *Gannett* decision as another example of the allegedly anti-press rulings of the Supreme Court. Allen H. Neuharth, chairman of the Gannett Company and president of the American Newspaper Publishers Association, said that the decision was "another chilling demonstration that the Burger Court is determined to unmake the Constitution. . . . It is the Supreme Court saying that the judiciary is a private judicial club, which can shut the door and conduct public business in private." Jack C. Landau, head of the Reporters Committee for Freedom of the Press, called the decision "judicial censorship of the rankest kind." The First Amendment, he said, did not give the judiciary the "power to decide what is newsworthy in their courts."

The *Gannett* decision was followed by an increase in attempts to close courtrooms to the public and press, according to a survey conducted by the Reporters Committee. The survey, made public August 4, 1979, listed more than thirty cases since July 2 in which motions were filed to exclude the press and/or the public from criminal trials or pretrial hearings. The committee found that the press and/or public had been closed out of courtroom proceedings in eighteen cases since July 2. In another ten cases, the attempts of judges to seal off their courtrooms had been overturned on appeal. Seven of the cases were in the full-trial stage.

The survey also reported that:

(a) Most of the motions for closure were made on the ground of avoiding publicity that might be prejudicial. The motions in at least two cases, however, cited a need to avoid "embarrassing" defendants, plaintiffs or witnesses. In a Virginia case, a judge had closed his courtroom to the press on the ground that it could not accommodate large numbers of reporters.

(b) Defense attorneys filed the majority of the closure motions, but prosecutors frequently joined in or filed their own motions to keep out the public and press.

(c) There have been at least three cases in which judges had allowed the public to view proceedings but had barred representatives of the press. In another case, a judge had permitted members of the press to attend a pretrial hearing but had forbidden them to report on it.

(d) Motions to bar the press from other aspects of trials, including the sentencing stage, were on the rise.

Chief Justice Burger, in a rare interview, indicated August 8 that judges who used the *Gannett* decision to close off trials had misread the Supreme Court ruling. Burger made his comments to the Gannett News Service during a visit to Flagstaff, Arizona. He said that the *Gannett* opinion "referred to pretrial proceedings only." He suggested that judges who barred the public or press from fullscale trials had "read newspaper reports of what we said" but had failed to consult the decision itself.

Justice Powell, participating in a panel discussion August 13 at the annual meeting of the American Bar Association in Dallas, Texas, said that the ruling was "based solely on the Sixth Amendment" right of defendants to a fair trial. The question of the right of the press to attend pretrial hearings under the First Amendment "was not reached" by the majority in the ruling, Powell said.

Exactly one year after the *Gannett* decision, the Supreme Court July 2, 1980 ruled, 7-1, that "absent an overriding interest," judges had no right to bar the public and press from criminal trials. In the case of *Richmond Newspapers* v. *Virginia,* the U.S. Supreme Court overturned a decision of the Virginia Supreme Court barring reporters for newspapers owned by Richmond Newspapers, Inc. from a 1979 murder trial.

Chief Justice Burger, author of the ruling opinion, held that access to criminal trials was guaranteed by the First and Fourteenth Amendments. Burger indicated that judges could close criminal trials under extraordinary circumstances, which they would be required to explain in writing. Justice Blackmun, concurring, called it "gratifying to see the court wash away at least some of the graffiti that marred the prevailing opinion in *Gannett*." Justice Stevens, concurring, noted that this was the first time the Supreme Court had "squarely held that the acquisition of newsworthy matter is entitled to any constitutional protection whatsoever." Justice Rehnquist, the sole dissenter, criticized the majority for interfering in the actions of a state judiciary.

In September 1980, the Judicial Conference of the United States, the top policymaking group for the federal judiciary, adopted a guideline providing that pretrial hearings in criminal cases "be held in open court" unless the trial judge found "a reasonable likelihood" that the accused's rights would be damaged and that his rights could be protected by no "reasonable alternatives" to closure. The conference's commentary, accompanying the guideline, said that the rule was designed to make sure that pretrial proceedings would be closed only in "very limited circumstances and only upon a proper showing of necessity." The commentary said that the guideline did not apply to the actual trials. The guideline was adopted in Washington D.C. at the Judicial Conference's semi-annual meeting.

Gagging the Press

In the effort to keep pretrial publicity from prejudicing juries, some judges have resorted to "gag orders," which forbid the publication (or broadcast) of specific information about cases scheduled for trial. Such orders obviously conflict with interpretations of the First Amendment's free-press guarantee as well as with the earlier British common-law right described thus in *Blackstone's Commentaries:* "The liberty of the press . . . consists in laying no *previous* restraint upon publication. . . ."

Thomas I. Emerson asserts in *The System of Freedom of Expression* that "[w]hen the First Amendment was adopted in 1791 it was clearly meant to outlaw any system of prior restraint. . . . There was indeed some who argued that this was all the First Amendment was intended to do." A case involving prior restraint did not reach the Supreme court, however, until 1931. Writing for the majority in this case (*Near* v. *Minnesota*), Chief Justice Charles Evans Hughes held that "the chief purpose of the First Amendment's guaranty is to prevent previous restraints on publication." The principle of "immunity from previous restraint," Hughes asserted, may be limited "only in exceptional cases." Emerson pointed out that in the *Near* ruling, "the court left in considerable confusion the question of what exceptions, if any, should be permitted to the prior restraint doctrine."

In 1976, in the case of *Nebraska Press Association* v. *Stuart,* the Supreme Court reaffirmed what then-Senator John V. Tunney asserted (in his preface to the Senate Constitutional Rights Subcommittee staff report on "Free Press-Fair Trial") was "its traditional hostility to prior restraints upon the press." Yet, Tunney noted, "the Court stopped short of adopting a general rule banning all prior restraints on the press on the fair trial context. . . ."

In the *Nebraska Press Association* matter, the Supreme Court June 29, 1976 unanimously voided a Nebraska judge's order barring pretrial news coverage of a mass-murder case. The press association had appealed the gag order, and the case had won national attention as a basic test of the conflicting guarantees of free press and of fair trial by unprejudiced jurors. The gag order, issued by Lincoln County District Judge Hugh Stuart, had prohibited pretrial publication of various items of information, including the existence of a confession by Erwin Charles Simants, who was accused of killing six members of a family in Sutherland, Nebraska October 18, 1975. The gag order prohibited publication of statements by the defendant, medical testimony and identities of victims of alleged sexual assaults. In addition, the order incorporated voluntary trial coverage guidelines worked out by judges, attorneys and the news media in Nebraska. Some of the prohibited information had been acquired by reporters in open courtroom proceedings.

Although all of the Supreme Court justices were in agreement that Stuart's order was unwarranted, they were divided on the question of whether orders like it could ever be imposed legitimately. The majority opinion, written by Chief Justice Warren E. Burger, and joined by Justices Harry A. Blackmun, Lewis F. Powell, Jr., William H. Rehnquist and Byron R. White, held that "guarantees of freedom of expression are not an absolute prohibition [of gag orders] under all circumstances, but the barriers to prior restraint remain high, and the presumption against its use continues intact." The decision described "prior restraints on speech and publication" as "the most serious and least tolerable infringement on First Amendment rights." In this particular case, Burger and the other justices in the majority held that the circumstances did not justify the restraining order. Burger noted that judges seeking to preserve a defendant's right to a fair trial against the impact of adverse publicity had a variety of recourses besides gag orders. Judges could delay a trial or order a change of venue, Burger said.

In a separate but concurring opinion, Justice William J. Brennan, Jr., joined by Justices Thurgood Marshall and Potter Stewart, went further. Brennan argued that "resort to prior restraints on the freedom of the press is a constitutionally impermissible method" of insuring a person's right to a fair trial. Justice John Paul Stevens, in another concurring opinion, held that gag orders could not be issued to suppress publication of information already "in the public domain." Stevens reserved judgment, however, on the admissibility of gag orders to suppress information that was obtained illegally, that invaded privacy or was "demonstrably false." White, although adhering to the majority opinion, said in a separate statement that he had "grave doubt . . . whether orders with respect to the press such as were entered in this case would ever be justifiable."

In an earlier development of the case, Blackmun November 21, 1975 had upheld portions of Judge Stuart's order. Acting in his capacity as the justice assigned to handle emergency motions from the Eighth U.S. judicial circuit, in which Nebraska fell, Blackmun ruled that a judge could forbid the print and broadcast media to report on confessions and a defendant's criminal record if the judge considered the order necessary to insure a fair trial. Blackmun stayed the order's adoption of the guidelines worked out for the state's press, but he added that the state courts would be free to reimpose provisions of the guidelines "so long as they are deemed pertinent to the facts of this particular case and so long as they are adequately specific. . . ." The associate justice found no justification for parts of the order prohibiting reporting of details of the crime, identities of the victims and medical testimony at an open preliminary hearing. Blackmun added that he was affirming the restriction on reporting of confessions as well as the ban on reporting by the news media that it had been ordered not to report the imposition of the gag order.

The Nebraska Supreme Court, acting December 1 at Blackmun's behest, unanimously upheld partial censorship of pretrial coverage in the Simants case. The state court ruled that the media could not report "information strongly implicative of the accused as the perpetrator of the slayings." Moreover, the court said that in future criminal cases, pretrial proceedings could be partly or entirely closed to the press and the public when, in the opinion of the presiding judge, the defendant's right to a fair trial would otherwise be impaired.

An increase in gag orders was reported May 8, 1976 by Jack Landau of the Reporters Committee for Freedom of the Press. Speaking at the annual meeting of the Louisiana-Mississippi Associated Press Association in New Orleans, Landau asserted that gag orders were "getting worse." He described three types of such curbs: Orders forbidding reporters to publish information they get in a court, orders sealing courtrooms and barring entry to newsmen, and orders prohibiting people involved in a court action to talk to reporters. Landau, a Newhouse Newspapers employee, asked: "Can any trial judge reasonably say today if you publish a story tomorrow that a defendant won't get a fair trial a few months from now?" He answered: "No, he can't."

Richard Schmidt, general counsel of the American Society of Newspaper Editors, addressed the same meeting. "The courts cannot be allowed to take over the job of editing newspapers," he declared but "that's what they're doing with gag orders." "If it comes to a choice between privacy and a free press," said Schmidt, "privacy must yield to a free press and free speech."

Acting in one of the gag-order controversies, Supreme Court Justice Powell July 24, 1974 had set aside an order by a New Orleans criminal court judge prohibiting the city's newspapers from reporting open-court testimony in a local rape-murder trial. Judge Oliver P. Schulingkamp had ordered the press not to print anything about the trial that might influence jurors. Schulingkamp's order covered interviews with witnesses, criminal records or confessions of the defendants, editorial comment before and during the trial and leaks suggesting the guilt or innocence of the accused. Schulingkamp had thus placed an unconstitutional prior restraint on freedom of the press, Powell said.

In Tennessee, *Monroe County Observer* editor Dan Hicks, Jr. was sentenced to five days in jail and was fined fifty dollars by County Judge J. P. Kennedy in Madisonville July 11, 1975 on a charge of contempt of court for publishing an article about a youth accused of murder. Kennedy suspended Hicks' sentence two and a half hours later. Hicks had charged in his weekly newspaper that the judge's "so-called order" prohibiting him from printing anything in regard to the June 23 slaying "would put me under effective censorship."

A Superior Court judge in Boston December 22, 1975 issued an order prohibiting the media from publishing the record of Susan Saxe, a former student radical, until a jury was chosen to hear her case. Judge Walter McLaughlin specifically barred the use of such phrases as "self-styled revolutionary," and ordered reporters not to mention that the accused had been sought by the Federal Bureau of Investigation for four and a half years for alleged involvement in the shooting of a policeman. Arrested March 27, she had pleaded guilty in Philadelphia June 9 to bank robbery and to theft from a federal arsenal.

The Supreme Court March 7, 1977, without recorded dissent, invalidated a gag order imposed by an Oklahoma court in the 1976 manslaughter trial of an eleven-year-old boy. The high court had stayed the gag order November 24, 1976. Acting in the case of *Oklahoma Publishing Co. v. District Court,* the Supreme Court ruled, in effect that the news media had a First Amendment right to publish information about juvenile defendants, providing that the information was acquired in public judicial proceedings. In granting the November 1976 stay, which temporarily nullified the gag order, the high court had noted that the minor's name and picture had already been "made available to the public as a result of a hearing held at the outset which was in fact open to the press." The gag order had previously been upheld by the Oklahoma Supreme Court. The latter court had held that the press' First Amendment right to freedom from prior restraint was outweighed by "the right of the juvenile to be spared from lifelong devastating effects of publicity for what might have been one irresponsible act."

In a further fine-tuning of the prior-restraint rules, the Supreme Court April 17, 1978 declined to review, and thus let stand, a lower court decision allowing a federal judge to isolate some evidence from the press during the trial of a former public official. The case, *Miami Herald Publishing Co. v. U.S.,* involved the actions of U.S. District Court Judge Ben Krentzman during the 1975 trial of former Florida Senator Edward J. Gurney. The Gurney trial, which concerned bribery and perjury charges, was covered extensively by newspapers in Miami and St. Petersburg. Krentzman said he feared that there might be a "bare possibility" that the unsequestered jurors might read about the trial in the newspapers. He therefore ordered that exhibits not yet admitted in evidence be kept from reporters and that transcripts of his conferences with the attorneys in the case be denied to the press. (Gurney was acquitted of a total of seven felony charges in the two trials, one in 1975, the other in 1976.) The judge's limitations on the press were challenged by a group of newspapers in the Fifth U.S. Circuit Court of Appeals. The newspapers argued that Krentzman had violated their First Amendment rights. The appeals court ruled in 1977 that the amendment did not protect against "incidental burdens on newsgathering" occurring in the case. The court contended that Krentzman had "employed reasonable 'remedials measures' far short of prior restraints, to prevent possible prejudice and maintain an orderly trial." By declining to review, the Supreme Court upheld this finding.

A clear ban on gag orders in the federal courts was adopted in September 1980 by the Judicial conference of the United States, the policymaking body for the federal judiciary. The guideline, approved by the Judicial Conference in Washington, D.C. at its semiannual meeting, bars orders by judges "which would prohibit representatives of the news media from broadcasting or publishing any information in their possession relating to a criminal case." The guideline conformed to the *Nebraska Press Association* ruling.

Protection of Sources

Does the Media Have a Right to Safeguard Confidentiality?

There is another issue that often involves free-press rights and the right to a fair trial. Much of the media insists that newsmen should not be required by courts or other government inquisitors to identify sources of confidential information or to surrender either their notes or information given to them in confidence. Television newsmen, largely supported by the rest of the media, assert that their unedited or unbroadcast tapes should also be immune to subpoena. Various court and investigative interests deny these media claims for reasons that are broader than concern for fair trial.

There are strong arguments for both positions.

The media usually asserts that the First Amendment, implicitly if not explicitly, protects newsmen from government efforts to make them disclose sources or confidential information. This protection is held to be part of the meaning of the term "free press." It is pointed out that much investigative reporting depends on informants who reveal their knowledge to reporters only on the promise that their identities would be kept secret.

Informants often have much to lose by being unmasked. In the cases of those who tell reporters the secrets of terrorist groups or of organized crime, their very lives can be at stake. Employees of government or business firms risk losing their jobs, their promotions or their careers when they tell newsmen about corruption by their superiors.

Many informants, therefore, would refuse to give their inside knowledge to reporters if they did not get a promise that they would not be identified. If government officials could force newsmen to name such tattlers, the media asserts, this important source of information would "dry out," and the public would be the major loser. It is said that under such conditions, the press would not be free.

Many lawyers argue, however, that First Amendment rights should not—and do not—always outweigh other rights. Some media people agree. When an accused person is on trial, with life or liberty at stake, this position is serious enough to cause questioning as to which rights should prevail. It is generally agreed that, with few exceptions, nobody with knowledge bearing on a case has the right to defy the courts and withhold his information. The Sixth Amendment provides that "In all criminal prosecutions, the accused shall enjoy the right . . . to be confronted with the witnesses against him; to have compulsory process for obtaining witnesses in his favor . . . . " When a reporter has found knowledgeable sources—in effect, potential witnesses—and has learned from them facts that may bear on the guilt or innocence of somebody on trial, does the First Amendment cancel the Sixth Amendment requirement that he obey court orders to identify his sources or surrender his investigative notes? To many people involved in criminal law, the answer is "no." Further, when a reporter has developed sources and information involving public safety or other important public interests, do legislative investigating committees or other government bodies have the right to force him to reveal his sources and knowledge? Members of such investigative bodies have often answered, in effect, "yes."

There are several types of confidential relationships that are accepted traditionally as justifying protection against forced disclosure of communications. These include the relationships between husband and wife, between attorney and client, between priest and penitent and between fellow jurors. The newsman's-shield controversy is an argument over assertions that, under the First Amendment's command, the relationship between reporter and informant should be added to this list.

The controversy is debated to a great extent on the basis of the conditions that might justify a privilege against forced disclosures

Protection of Sources

by people with specific relationships to each other. Four fundamental conditions, as listed in J. Wigmore on *Evidence,* are widely recognized as esesntial to establishing such a privilege. These are: "(1) The communications must originate in a *confidence* that they will not be disclosed; (2) This element of *confidentiality must be essential* to the full and satisfactory maintenance of the relation between the parties; (3) the *relation* must be one which in the opinion of the community ought to be sedulously *fostered*; and (4) The *injury* that would inure to the relation by the disclosure . . . must be *greater than the benefit* thereby gained for the correct disposal or litigation."

Dierdre Carmody commented in *The New York Times* July 28, 1978 that, in the general view of the media, "the very functioning of a free press will begin to wither" if reporters are forced to surrender information they develop. This opinion echoed views expressed by many other journalists. The framers of the Constitution, Carmody held, "meant the press to be a kind of overseer of government" that would freely report on "what the government was actually doing." Newsmen can perform this function only by assuring their "informants within the government . . . that their identities will not be made public," Carmody wrote. She added that the framers intended the press "to be separate from the government" but that the press would become nothing more than an instrument of the courts" if judges could force reporters to reveal all data they acquired. She cited "the view of the framers" in asserting that "the press should not become an investigative arm of the government."

The issue had been taken up at a White House press conference April 29, 1971. President Richard M. Nixon told reporters that he took "a very jaundiced view" of "subpoenaing the notes of reporters" or "government action which requires the revealing of sources . . . unless it is strictly—and this would be a very narrow area—strictly in the area where there was a major crime that had been committed and where the subpoenaing of the notes had to do with information dealing directly with that crime."

For many reporters, the keeping of confidences is a matter of professional honor regardless of their rights under the First Amendment. In 1934 the American Newspaper Guild adopted a canon of ethics requiring "That newspapermen shall refuse to reveal confidences or disclose sources of confidential information in courts or before other judicial or investigatory bodies, and that the newspaperman's duty to keep confidences shall include those he shared with one employer after he has changed his employment."

Charles A. Perlik, Jr., president of the Newspaper Guild, told the Senate Constitutional Rights Subcommittee February 16, 1972 that, in the Guild's view, newsmen had an "absolute and unqualified right" to "protect their information and matierals as well as their sources from forced disclosure" and that this right "applies to any information or source, confidential or not." "Demands for disclosure of newsmen's notes, tapes, films, photographs or files, or for disclosure of their sources, whether made by the government or by private persons, endanger the trust between newsman and news source," the statement said. "And that trust is essential both to the ability of the press to provide the public the information to which it has a right under the First Amendment and to the newsman's ability to carry out his function under the First Amendment."

The history of this controversy "goes back to President George Washington's jailing of a correspondent for refusing to tell the Senate his source for the publication of a proposed treaty between the United States and Mexico." This historical note was inserted by Congressman Glenn M. Anderson, a California Democrat, in the March 7, 1973 issue of the *Congressional Record*. Anderson noted that "in the first 190 years of our nation, in only four out of eighty cases have newsmen yielded to judicial pressure and revealed their sources."

The press has also resisted Congressional pressure as early as 1857, when reporter James Simonton indicated in an article in *The New York Times* that members of Congress had taken bribes. A select committee of the House of Representatives ordered Simonton to reveal his sources. Simonton refused to commit what he described as a dishonorable betrayal of confidence, and he was found in contempt of Congress.

American newsmen have also protected sources when working abroad. A.M. Rosenthal of *The New York Times* told a House Judiciary subcommittee March 6, 1973 that in 1959 he had been expelled from Poland "on the charge of probing too deeply into the internal affairs of the government, the party and the leadership." "Every bit of information I received came from Poles who trusted my word that I would protect them," he testified. ". . . If I had been called into a Polish court and asked to reveal who told me what, I believe that every member of Congress would have supported my refusal to testify had I had the strength to do so.

"And I was by no means the only foreign correspondent who found himself in this kind of situation. It happens all the time. Henry Raymont . . . was arrested in Cuba and grilled as to the sources of his information having to do with the Bay of Pigs. Mr. Raymont was even threatened with execution, but he did not reveal his sources. And now, fourteen years later, we have a debate in our country on whether an American newsman has the right to do and act in our own society as I did in a Communist society—to inquire, to write, to protect his sources and information and thus his existence as a conveyor of information to the public . . . . "

The *Los Angeles Times* January 14, 1973 quoted John Hohenberg, secretary of the Pulitzer Prize Advisory Board, as saying that "every Pulitzer Prize won for coverage of the Vietnam War, beginning with those won by Malcolm Browne of the AP and David Halberstam of *The New York Times* in 1964, depended on confidential sources."

An apparent change in judicial attitudes toward newsmen's rights was suggested by Johnny H. Killian of the Legislative Reference Service of the Library of Congress. This change appeared to favor at least a limited newsman's privilege. Some court decisions later in the 1970s did not entirely support this evaluation. In a report inserted in the March 25, 1971 issue of the *Congressional Record,* Killian noted that so far "the greatest number of freedom-of-the-press cases are far removed from supporting any argument relating to a constitutionally-required newsman's privilege." He pointed out that "compulsory disclosure of sources is not designed to abridge news gathering or to operate as a prior restraint on publishing or to punish the news media for disseminating certain materials. . . . And inasmuch as many of the cases proceed upon the basis that newsmen and their employers are guaranteed certain basic rights in carrying on their business, the imposition of a duty to testify which is in the main applicable to all other persons seems no more than the placing of a burden on them which all of us share."

"But," Killian continued, "a number of recent cases have appeared to read the First Amendment in a somewhat different fashion than the older cases did; whereas the older cases in the main read the amendment as containing a series of 'thou shalt nots' directed at the government, the newer cases have also included suggestions that the amendment contains a series of 'must do' commandments directed at government . . . . In good part, these cases reflect a philosophy that what the First Amendment guarantees is not the freedom of the news media and other disseminators of information and entertainment to carry on their business as they choose but rather the right of the people to be informed about those things which affect them."

If the First Amendment interpretation were expanded to mean assurance "that the public is adequately informed," Killian wrote, "the balance which might be drawn between the duty of everyone to testify and the privilege of newsmen to conceal their sources might well be differently weighed. If compelled testimony might in certain cases so injure the ability of newsmen to inform the public, then a privilege might be recognized in those cases."

By 1970 the media had already been gaining wide support in a campaign against forcing newsmen to disclose sources or confidential information, and the Nixon Administration made some attempt to pacify the media. A Department of Justice spokesman said February 7, 1970 that Attorney General John N. Mitchell had offered to meet with media representatives to dispel their fears that the government was using its subpoena powers excessively. This offer followed a series of subpoenas issued to newsmen who were covering the activities of radical political groups.

The first of these subpoenas had been served on the Columbia Broadcasting System (CBS) January 8 for the out-takes (unused portions) of a film dealing with the activities of the Black Panther Party. CBS was served January 29 with a second subpoena demanding that the network turn over to the Secret Service and the Federal Bureau of Investigation (FBI) a complete record of all the materials used to produce the film, including the recorded tapes of an interview with Eldridge Cleaver, the party's self-exiled "minister of information." Representatives of *Time, Life* and *Newsweek* magazines revealed February 1 that the government had subpoenaed their unedited files and unused photographs dealing with the movements of the militant Weatherman faction of Students for a Democratic Society (SDS) during four days of civil disturbances in Chicago October 8-11, 1969. Spokesmen for three magazines said that the subpoenas were served shortly after the disorders. *The New York Times* reported February 2 that one of its reporters, Earl Caldwell, had been subpoenaed to testify before a federal grand jury investigating the activities of the Black Panthers. The subpoena directed Caldwell to appear before the grand jury with his "notes and tape recordings" regarding Panther activities and personnel.

Executives representing the *Times,* CBS, *Time* and *Newsweek* February 4 issued statements assailing the government's apparent policy of using subpoenas to collect information from news organizations about radical political groups. Attorney General Mitchell said February 5 that the Department of Justice was taking steps to assure the media that subpoenas would not be issued to newsmen without an attempt first to reach agreement on the scope of the subpoenas.

Mike Wallace, the CBS-TV news correspondent, said February 23 that the Department of Justice had asked him to testify voluntarily before a federal grand jury in New Haven, Connecticut in an investigation of Black Panther activities. This was the third time the government had sought data on the Panthers from CBS personnel and news files. Wallace had interviewed Eldridge Cleaver for a January 6 telecast. Wallace said that Paul Loewenwater, the producer of the January 6 telecast, was also asked to appear before the grand jury. A spokesman for the Department of Justice confirmed February 21 that contacts had been made with some CBS people, and he acknowledged the possibility of serving subpoenas on them. The spokesman said that Attorney General Mitchell did not think the contacts conflicted with his February 5 statement that no further subpoenas would be issued to people associated with national media without a preliminary attempt to negotiate an agreement on their scope.

The media's objections to the subpoenas were supported February 12 by Federal Communications Commissioner Nicholas Johnson. Johnson said that the media had an "absolute right" to refuse the demands of government invetigators for reporters' confidential information and unused television film. He assailed the Nixon Administration and the Department of Justice for what he termed a "wave of government subpoenas . . . ." Johnson charged that the subpoenas, "together with other manipulations of the press, have placed the freedom and integrity of this country's news media in serious jeopardy." He also criticized the media's management for what he called its "acquiescence."

Mitchell August 10, 1970 issued guidelines to the Department of Justice that barred government lawyers from seeking subpoenas to force testimony from newsmen in criminal cases without his personal approval. In a speech in St. Louis before the House of Delegates of the American Bar Association, Mitchell said that the guidelines "represent a genuine effort . . . to acommodate the respective responsibilities of the news media and the federal prosecutor." He acknowledged that some disputed subpoenas had been issued "in haste," withouit considering the effects on freedom of the press, but he also asserted that the department would retain its right to use the subpoena where "fair administration of justice requires it." The guidelines warned that if subpoenas were obtained without prior approval by the attorney general, the department would move to quash the subpoena. Under the new rules, in considering use of the subpoena, the government was to balance the possible infringement on the exercise of First Amendment rights against the public interest in justice. All reasonable attempts were to be made to obtain information from non-press sources before a subpoena would be issued. The guidelines also required negotiations with newsmen before resorting to the subpoena. The guidelines included the following principles: that the press should not be used as a "springboard" for investigations, and subpoenas should be used only if a crime were indicated by sources outside the media; the subpoena should be used only to secure essential information that the government had tried unsuccessfully to get from non-press sources; normally, the subpoena should be used only for the verification of published information, and great caution should be observed when unpublished material was involved; and material sought should be of a limited nature—in subject matter, time covered and volume.

Some three years later a subsequent attorney general, Elliot Richardson, used Mitchell's guidelines as the basis of an expanded "statement of policy" that he issued October 16, 1973 on "the issuance of subpoenas to, and the interrogation, indictment, or arrest of, members of the news media." A departmental memorandum issued March 1, 1973 had noted that "Since August 1970 there have been eleven situations in which newsmen, while they were willing to testify or produce documents, preferred that a subpoena be issued . . . . In only two of the thirteen situations in which subpoenas have been requested of newsmen was a confidential source involved, and in both of these situations the information was supplied on the basis of an agreement with the newsman."

The Caldwell, Branzburg & Pappas Cases

The case of *New York Times* reporter Earl Caldwell worked its way through the courts for two years. The Supreme Court finally ruled, in a decision lumping the Caldwell matter with two similar cases, that there was no First Amendment "privilege" permitting a reporter "to refuse to answer the relevant and material questions asked during a good-faith grand jury investigation." Therefore, the court held, "there is no privilege to refuse to appear before such a grand jury until the government demonstrates some 'compelling need' for a newsman's testimony."

The first court ruling in the Caldwell case had been announced April 9, 1970 when U.S. District Court Judge Alfonzo J. Zirpoli in San Francisco signed an order limiting the government's power to subpoena Caldwell. The order was issued after an April 3 hearing at which Caldwell's attorneys asked for the quashing of the subpoena requiring Caldwell to appear before the grand jury investigating the Black Panther Party. Zirpoli held that Caldwell should not be required to disclose confidential information or sources developed in his news-gathering work. The order specifically protected Caldwell's right to defend his confidential relationships with Black Panther leaders as news sources. Zirpoli declined to cancel the subpoena, but he ordered that Caldwell be permitted to consult his attorney during his testimony before the grand jury. The judge also left open to the government the right to prove in a new hearing that the national interest required Caldwell's testimony on the ground that the information he had acquired could be obtained in no other way. Zirpoli restated his opinion that Caldwell and his employers had legal standing to resist the attempt to subpoena confidential information from him. The judge said that to require testimony from Caldwell based on his confidential relationships with his sources would "damage and impair" the professional activities of other *Times* reporters and of other news agencies.

Caldwell then refused to appear before the grand jury, and Zirpoli June 5 found him guilty of civil contempt. The U.S. Circuit Court of Appeals for the Ninth Circuit, however, vacated the contempt judgment November 16 and reversed Zirpoli's order requiring Caldwell to present himself before the grand jury. The appeals court said that the government must demonstrate that evidence is necessary and otherwise unobtainable before a newsman can be forced to submit to grand jury questioning. "Where it has been shown that the public's First Amendment right to be informed would be jeopardized by requiring a journalist to submit to secret grand jury interrogation," the appeals court held, "the government must respond by demonstrating a compelling need for the witnesses' presence before judicial process properly can issue to require attendance." The appeals court conceded that the Caldwell case was unique in that "it is not every news source that is as sensitive as the Black Panther Party. . . . It is not every reporter who so uniquely enjoys the trust and confidence of his sensitive news source."

The appeals court ruled that if "the grand jury may require appellant [Caldwell] to make available to it information obtained by him in his capacity as news gatherer, then the grand jury and the Department of Justice have the power to appropriate appellant's investigative efforts to their own behalf—to convert him after the fact into an investigative agent of the government. The very concept of a free press requires that the news media be accorded a measure of autonomy; that they should be free to pursue their own investigations to their own ends without fear of governmental interference; and that they should be able to protect their investigative processes. To convert news gatherers into Department of Justice investigators is to invade the autonomy of the press by imposing a governmental function upon them. To do so where the result is to diminish their future capacity as news gatherers is destructive to their public function. To accomplish this where it has not been shown to be essential to the grand jury inquiry simply cannot be justified in the public interest."

The appellate judgment held that "the relationship between journalists and news sources depends upon a trust and confidence that is constantly subject to reexamination and that depends in turn on actual knowledge of how news and information imparted have been handled and on continuing reassurance that the handling has been discreet. This reassurance disappears when the reporter is called to testify behind closed doors. The secrecy that surrounds grand jury testimony necessarily introduces uncertainty in the minds of those who fear betrayal of their confidence."

The appeals court decision was overturned by a 5-4 Supreme Court ruling June 29, 1972. The matter of *United States, Peti-*

Protection of Sources

tioner, v. *Earl Caldwell* was decided in a ruling that included the decisions in the cases of *Paul M. Branzburg* v. *John P. Hayes, Judge, etc. et al.* and *In the Matter of Paul Pappas, Petitioner.* Justice Bryon R. White, author of the majority opinion, wrote that "the issue in these cases is whether requiring newsmen to appear and testify before state or federal grand juries abridges the freedom of speech and press guaranteed by the First Amendment." "We hold that it does not," White asserted. The syllabus (summarizing the decision) said: "The First Amendment does not relieve a newspaper reporter of the obligation that all citizens have to respond to a grand jury subpoena and answer questions relevant to a criminal investigation, and therefore the Amendment does not afford him a constitutional testimonial privilege for an agreement he makes to conceal the criminal conduct of his source or evidence thereof."

Branzburg was a reporter for the Louisville (Ky.) *Courier-Journal.* In a by-line story appearing in his paper's November 15, 1969 issue, he had reported on how two residents of Jefferson County, Ky. synthesized hashish from marihuana. On the basis of this article, he was subpoenaed by the Jefferson County grand jury and was asked to identify the two hashish makers. Branzburg refused. He was then ordered by a state trial court judge (Judge J. Miles Pound) to answer the grand jury's questions, and he again refused. The judge and the Kentucky Court of Appeals denied that his refusal to answer was authorized by the Kentucky reporters' privilege statute. In a second article, published January 10, 1971, Branzburg described interviews with and observations of dozens of "drug users" in Frankfort, Ky. A Franklin County, Ky. grand jury subpoenaed him to testify about what he had seen. Both the lower court and the Kentucky Court of Appeals denied his request to quash the subpoena.

Pappas, a television newsman-photographer, was in Bedford, Mass. July 30, 1970 to cover civil disorders. The Black Panthers allowed him to enter their headquarters in Bedford on his promise not to disclose anything he saw or heard there except what would happen during an anticipated police raid. Since the raid did not take place, Pappas wrote no story and revealed none of the things he saw in the Panther headquarters. Two months later he was summoned before the Bristol County Grand Jury. He testified about events outside the Panther headquarters but refused to tell what had taken place inside. A second summons was issued, and his motion to quash it was denied by both the trial judge and the Supreme Judicial Court of Massachusetts.

"The sole issue before us," White wrote in the majority opinion on the three cases, "is the obligation of reporters to respond to grand jury subpoenas as other citizens do and to answer questions relevant to an investigation into the commission of crime. . . . [N]either the First Amendment nor other constitutional provision protects the average citizen from disclosing to a grand jury information that he has received in confidence. The claim is, however, that reporters are exempt from these obligations because if forced to respond to subpoenas and identify their sources or disclose other confidences, their informants will refuse or be reluctant to furnish newsworthy information in the future. This asserted burden on news gathering is said to make compelled testimony from newsmen constitutionally suspect and to require a privilege position for them.

"It is clear that the First Amendment does not invalidate every incidental burdening of the press that may result from the enforcement of civil or criminal statutes of general applicability. Under prior cases, otherwise valid laws serving substantial interests may be enforced against the press as against others, despite the possible burden that may be imposed . . . . The prevailing view is that the press is not free with impunity to publish everything and anything it desires to publish . . . .

"It has generally been held that the First Amendment does not guarantee the press a constitutional right of special access to information not available to the public generally. . . . In *Zemel* v. *Rusk* [1965] . . . for example, the [Supreme] Court sustained the government's refusal to validate passports to Cuba even though that restriction 'rendered less than wholly free the flow of information concerning that country.' . . . The ban on travel was held constitutional, for '[t]he right to speak and publish does not carry with it the unrestrained right to gather information.' . . .

"Despite the fact that news gathering may be hampered, the press is regularly excluded from grand jury proceedings, our own [Supreme Court] conferences, the meetings of other official bodies gathered in executive session, and the meetings of private organizations. Newsmen have no constitutional right of access to the scenes of crime or disaster when the general public is excluded, and they may be prohibited from attending or publishing infor-

Protection of Sources 165

mation about trials if such restrictions are necessary to assure a defendant a fair trial before an impartial tribunal. . . .

"It is thus not surprising that the great weight of authority is that newsmen are not exempt from the normal duty of appearing before a grand jury and answering questions relevant to a criminal investigation. At common law, courts consistently refused to recognize the existence of any privilege authorizing a newsman to refuse to reveal confidential information to a grand jury. . . .

". . . Until now the only testimonial privilege for unofficial witnesses that is rooted in the federal Constitution is the Fifth Amendment privilege agaisnt compelled self-incrimination. We are asked to create another by interpreting the First Amendment to grant newsmen a testimonial privilege that other citizens do not enjoy. This we decline to do. . . . W[e] perceive no basis for holding that the public interest in law enforcement and in ensuring effective grand jury proceedings is insufficient to override the consequential, but uncertain, burden on news gathering which is said to result from insisting that reporters . . . respond to relevant questions put to them in the course of a valid grand jury investigation or criminal trial. . . ."

Justice Potter Stewart, dissenting, criticized the finding that "a newsman has no First Amendment right to protect his sources when called before a grand jury." He warned that "the court thus invites state and federal authorities to undermine the historic independence of the press by attempting to annex the journalistic profession as an investigative arm of government. Not only will this decision impair performance of the press' constitutionally protected functions, but it will, I am convinced, in the long run, harm rather than help the administration of justice. . . ."

The court has "held that the right to publish is central to the First Amendment and basic to the existence of constitutional democracy," Stewart continued. ". . . A corollary of the right to publish must be the right to gather news. . . . The right to gather news implies, in turn, a right to a confidential relationship between a reporter and his source. This proposition follows as a matter of simple logic once three factual predicates are recognized: (1) newsmen require informants to gather news; (2) confidentiality—the promise or understanding that names or certain aspects of communications will be kept off the record— is essential to the creation and maintenance of a news-gathering relationship with informants; and (3) the existence of an unbridled subpoena power—the absence of a constitutional right protecting, in *any* way, a confidential relationship from compulsory process—will either deter sources from divulging information or deter reporters from gathering and publishing information. . . ."

In a further dissent, Justice William O. Douglas asserted that a "reporter is no better than his sources of information. Unless he has a privilege to withhold the identity of his source, he will be the victim of governmental intrigue or aggression. If he can be summoned to testify in secret before a grand jury, his sources will dry up and the attempted exposure, the effort to enlighten the public, will be ended. If what the court sanctions today becomes settled law, then the reporter's main function in American society will be to pass on to the public the press releases which the various departments of governmental issue."

Newmen's Shield Laws & the Jailing of Reporters

The controversy over efforts to make newsmen reveal their sources has led to scores of proposals to provide a legal "shield" to protect the media from such pressures. The first newsmen's shield law was adopted by the state of Maryland in 1896. Ultimately some eighteen other states enacted a variety of similar laws. The first federal bill for a newsmen's shield was introduced in the Senate in 1929 by the late Senator Arthur Capper, the Kansas Republican. An especially strong effort was made in the early 1970s to have Congress enact such legislation, but this campaign was unsuccessful.

Strong support for a federal newsmen's shield law was enunciated by most but not all media representatives who testified before Congressional committees or who otherwise made their views known.

Caution on the newsman's shield question was urged by *Detroit News* editor Martin S. Hayden in an October 4, 1971 letter to Senator Sam J. Ervin, chairman of the Senate Constitutional Rights Subcommittee. Hayden and *The Detroit News* "would prefer to have legislative bodies stay out of the newspaper business," Hayden wrote. "Certainly we want no new laws restricting present operations of the free American press and, in consistency's name, we carry that to the point of wariness about any legislation which would give special privilege to newspapers. Along this line we see some inconsistency in the more extreme positions of some of our colleagues who, while on the one hand defending a national 'right to know' which would make everyone else divulge information, seemingly would exempt 'responsible' editors and broadcasters from any required contribution to that public 'right.' The one very limited exception we would make is in the case of a newsman with a legitimate need to protect a confidential news source. . . . I favor a spelled-out and reasonably qualified legal statement of a newspaperman's privilege to protect confidential information. . . ." [V]arious states . . . have legislation protecting a reporter's right to maintain confidence. A similar privilege should, I believe, be extended to the federal system. . . . I reluctantly disagree with some of my editorial colleagues who seemingly would demand for the communications media a privilege going far beyond that now accorded to lawyers, ministers and doctors. A minister, for instance, who from his pulpit sees a crime committed in the midst of his congregation could not refuse to testify on the basis of the privilege surrounding information given to him in the confessional. . . . Similar limits . . . logically apply to a newspaper reporter. Sent out on a straight news assignment, he can hardly claim professional privilege of refusal to testify as to what he sees . . . . "

Senator Ervin summarized some of the arguments in the controversy February 20, 1973 as he opened a fresh series of hearings by the Senate Subcommittee on Constitutional Rights. "Our problem . . . is to decide whether or not to adopt some form of statutory protection [for newsmen] and, if so, what form that protection should take," he said. ". . . First of all, does the lack of a testimonial privilege for newsmen really present a problem? There has never been such a federal privilege before, and yet sources of information have obviously not 'dried up.' There has always been a threat that the newsman may be called before a court or grand jury and forced to reveal his sources. Yet certainly there has been continuing disclosure by informants since the beginning of the Republic. On the other hand, we will never know how much we might have known had not this threat of a press subpoena and ultimate exposure been hanging over the sources of confidential information. It does stand to reason that sources would be more reluctant to come forward and reporters more reluctant to publish when to do so may subject them to subpoena and an indeterminate jail sentence . . . . "

Ervin noted the "competing interests involved": "On the one

hand is society's interest in being informed—in learning of crime, corruption or mismanagement. . . . On the other hand, we have the pursuit of truth in the courtroom. It is the duty of every man to give testimony. The Sixth Amendment specificlaly gives a criminal defendant the right to confront the witnesses against him and to have compulsory process for obtaining witnesses in his favor. Society, too, has a marked interest in identifying and punishing the violators of its laws. All of this must necessarily be made more difficult by any testimonial privilege . . . . ''

Ervin also called attention to the fear "that such a testimonial privilege will become a shield behind which irresponsible journalists may hide. Without revealing source there is no means of evaluating the accuracy or fairness of news reporting, nor indeed whether the story is not a complete fabrication." Ervin quoted a letter he had received that asked: "How can the public judge the trustworthiness of news gathered . . . from anonymous informants or secret sources? Would not shield legislation encourage irresponsible newsmen to obtain information by theft or bribary? . . . What is to prevent a newsman from asserting truth as a defense in a libel suit and then refusing to tell who the source was? . . .''

Ervin added that "even some in the press have doubts about the wisdom of . . . [shield] legislation. They feel that . . . the First Amendment is an unequivocal guarantee of a free press which should not be tampered with. Any legislation must unavoidably have the effect of limiting that guarantee . . . . ''

The House of Delegates of the American Bar Association, by 157-122 vote February 4, 1974, rejected a proposal to support bills before Congess that would grant reporters the right to refuse to reveal confidential information to investigators, prosecutors or judges. Proponents of the shield-law resolution told the delegates that newsmen needed such a law to expose corruption in government. Warning that such a privilege would verge on the absolute and cover a wide and indistinct class, opponents argued that newsmen's privilege would encourage grand jury secrecy violations, hamper the ability of victims of libel to protect themselves against irresponsible reporting and ultimately cause the public to demand regulation of the press.

Supporters of a federal newsmen's shield law complain that state shield laws are largely ineffective. For example, New York's law, which went into effect in May 1970, was described by American Newspaper Guild President Charles A. Perlik, Jr. before the Senate Constitutional Rights Subcommittee February 16, 1972 as "considered to be among the most liberal laws in the privilege area." Under the New York law, however, the publisher of the *Village Voice* "was indeed forced to turn over an original manuscript," Perlik told the subcommittee.

The *Voice* article was identified as written by an inmate of the Manhattan House of Detention (the Tombs) who was later indicted on charges resulting from riots in the prison. State Supreme Court Justice Harold Birns, in an opinion published January 27, 1972, rejected the *Voice's* attempt to avoid a subpoena. His reason was that the manuscript involved, given to *Voice* reporter Mary Breasted, had been published under the by-line of the presumed author, Ricardo de Leon, and that there was no "cloak of confidentiality" involved. Birns' opinion said reporters had a right to withhold information and the identity of sources under the New York law only when they received the data with an understanding that the "information or its sources not be disclosed."

Critics of the *Village Voice* ruling pointed out that the New York law barred a contempt finding against a professional journalist for refusing "to disclose any news of the sources of any such news coming into his possession" while gathering news for broadcast or publication.

Following the June 29, 1972 Supreme Court ruling (in the *Caldwell, Branzburg* and *Pappas* cases) that newsmen had no Constitutional privilege against being required to make disclosures before a grand jury, several reporters chose to go to jail for contempt of court rather than identify sources or reveal information received in confidence.

Peter J. Bridge, former *Newark* (N.J.) *Evening News* reporter, surrendered in Newark October 4, 1972 to begin an indeterminate sentence for contempt. The Supreme Court had declined the previous day to stay Bridge's jailing after he refused to answer grand jury questions about an alleged bribe offer to a Newark Housing Authority official. The Supreme Court's 8-1 decision to deny an appeal by Bridge was disclosed to newsmen in a two-sentence statement. The statement said that Justice William O. Douglas would have granted the stay. Bridge had been sentenced for refusing to answer five questions asked by a county grand jury investigating corruption in the Newark Housing Authority. The questions he refused to answer dealt with the reported bribe attempt, what the bribe was for and whether any Newark housing officials had been harassed. The court held that since Bridge had already named his informant—Mrs. Pearl Beatty, the official who claimed that she had been offered a bribe—he had, in effect, waived his protection under New Jersey's shield law. Bridge served in jail a total of 20 days.

In reaction to the jailing of Bridge, the New Jersey legislature December 14, 1972 passed a law described as the nation's strongest state newsmen's privilege stature. The measure would allow anybody gathering news for any news media to refuse to disclose any information about the article or its sources to any judicial or investigative body, regardless of whether or not the information was actually published. A newsman would remain under the measure's protection even after he left the journalistic profession.

William T. Farr of of the *Los Angeles Times* was jailed November 16, 1972 for refusing to tell a Los Angeles Superior Court judge the identity of the source for an article he had written about the Charles Manson case in 1970. Released later November 16, pending an appeal, Farr was returned to prison November 27. He was finally released January 11, 1973, after 48 days in jail, under an order of Supreme Court Justice Douglas, pending a review of his case by a federal appeals court. Over Douglas' dissent, the Supreme Court earlier had refused to review a previous appeal by Farr. During the Manson trial, Farr had been protected by California's state newsmen's privilege law. When he left the *Los Angeles Herald-Examiner* after the trial, however, Judge Charles C. Older, who had presided at the trial, ordered him to reveal his sources and had jailed him when he refused. Kelleher also said that Farr's "lurid" articles demonstrated the "compelling need to protect the defendant against prejudicial publicity." (Governer Ronald Reagon December 30, 1972 signed a bill strengthening the California law that gave newsmen the right to withhold the identity of their sources from grand juries.)

Four *Fresno Bee* newsmen were jailed in Fresno, Calif. September 3, 1976 for refusing to identify the source of information for three articles published in the *Bee* in 1975. They were freed September 17 after Superior Court Judge Hollis Best, who had sentenced them to indefinite terms for contempt of court, ruled that keeping them in jail was pointless since all four had testified that they would not reveal the source. The journalists were managing editor George F. Gruner, ombudsman (and former city editor) James H. Bort, Jr. and reporters William K. Patterson and

Joe Rosato. It was reported that neither Gruner nor Bort knew the identity of the source that they had been jailed for protecting.

The *Bee* articles included excerpts from a grand jury transcript that had been ordered sealed by Superior Court Judge Denver C. Peckinpah. The case involved bribery indictments against a Fresno city councilman and two others. (The councilman was acquitted in a trial in Oakland after a change of venue.) Peckinpah had found the four newsmen guilty of contempt on seventy-six counts, and an appellate court upheld him on fifty-five counts. Judge Best pronounced the sentences after Peckinpah's retirement, and appeals were rejected by the California Supreme Court and the U.S. Supreme Court. In convicting the *"Bee* Four," Peckinpah ruled that California's newsman's shield law did not protect them because it did not apply when the order to reveal sources was issued by a judge.

While the newsmen were imprisoned, the Fresno County Courthouse was picketed in their support by about 150 California newsmen September 5 and by members of the Reverend Jim Jones' San Francisco church.

The Supreme Court October 31, 1977 declined to review a decision by the Idaho Supreme Court that a reporter could not withhold the identity of a confidential news source when called as a witness in a civil suit. The case, *Tribune Publishing Co.* v. *Caldero,* involved a libel suit against the *Lewiston Morning Tribune* by Michael A. Caldero, a former agent for the state Bureau of Narcotics & Organized Crime. Caldero had been fired by the bureau after an article in a 1973 issue of the *Morning Tribune* charged him with misconduct during a narcotics arrest. The article, written by reporter James E. (Jay) Shelledy, quoted an unnamed "police expert" as its source of information. Shelledy, who had been called as a witness in Caldero's libel suit, refused to reveal the identity of his source and was sentenced to thirty days in jail for contempt of court. His sentence was upheld by the Idaho Supreme Court.

New York Times reporter Myron A. Farber was sentenced by New Jersey Superior Court Judge Theodore W. Trautwein July 24, 1978 to an indefinite term in the Bergen County (N.J.) jail plus an additional six months. He and the *Times* had been found guilty of civil and criminal contempt of court for refusing to give Superior Court Judge William J. Arnold all their notes and files on the "Dr. X" case.

In the "Dr. X" affair, Farber in 1975 had investigated the mysterious deaths in 1965 and 1966 of thirteen patients at Riverdell Hospital in Oradell, N.J. His subsequent articles in the *Times* January 7 and 8, 1976 led to the murder trial of Dr. Mario E. Jascalevich in Hackensack, N.J. (Dr. Jascalevich, the "Dr. X" of Farber's articles, was acquitted October 24, 1978 of having killed three patients with curare injections.)

In imposing the indefinite jail term on Farber, Judge Trautwein ordered that Farber be held in jail until he produced the data subpoenaed. Farber was also fined $1,000 on the civil contempt charge and another $1,000 on the criminal contempt charge. The *Times* was simultaneously fined $100,000 July 24, 1978 plus $5,000 a day for every day it failed to produce the files as demanded.

Farber began his jail term August 4 but was released August 30 on orders of the New Jersey Supreme Court pending appeals of his and the Times' contempt convictions. Three weeks later the same court, in a 5-2 decision September 21, upheld the contempt citations. The court rejected the defense claim of Farber and the *Times* that the New Jersey press-shield law gave them the right to protect the identities of informants. According to the state Supreme Court, the shield law violated Jascalevich's Sixth Amendment right to a fair trial. Farber then returned to jail October 12 after the U.S. Supreme Court refused October 6 to review the state court decision and Farber October 10 again refused to give up his notes.

On the ending of Jascalevich's trial October 24, Judge Trautwein ordered Farber to be freed and the daily fines imposed on the *Times* to be ended. He said that since the trial was over, the need for Farber's notes no longer existed. Farber thus was released after spending a total of 38 days in jail; the *Times* paid a total of $289,000 in fines.

While Farber was still in jail, his attorneys had gone into U.S. District Court in Newark and filed a petition to free him under a writ of *habeas corpus*. Refusing to release the reporter, Federal Judge Frederick B. Lacey August 11 had criticized him for not having revealed that he had contracted with the publisher Doubleday & Company to write a book on the "Dr. X" case and had taken a $75,000 advance from Doubleday in 1976. The judge suggested that Farber was keeping his notes secret because of his financial interest in using them in the book. According to the judge, Farber would "profit handsomely" if Jascalevich were found guilty. Lacey called the situation "a sorry spectacle of a reporter standing on First Amendment principles, standing in sackcloth and ashes when in fact he is standing at the altar of greed."

The *Times* August 18 had surrendered its files on the case plus Farber's partially completed manuscript to Judge Arnold, but Farber continued to withhold his personal notes on the investigation. All but the manuscript and the personal notes had already been supplied to the court by a witness. Judge Trautwein August 28 described the files produced by the *Times* as "clearly and unequivocally sanitized." The sentence he had imposed remained in force until first suspended by the state Supreme Court and then ended by Trautwein himself on the conclusion of Jascalevich's trial.

Farber spent a total of more than a month in prison and the *Times* spent more than half a million dollars on legal fees and fines to defend the media's right to keep the identities of sources secret, specifically, the identity of Farber's informants in the "Dr. X" case. A *New York Times* article by Robert D. McFadden revealed November 28, 1978, however, that it was public relations executive Eileen Milling who had started Farber on his investigation by urging the *Times* to look into the matter.

The *Times* was ordered by Judge Trautwein August 14, 1979 to pay Jascalavich $1,700.38 for expenses accrued during the contempt proceedings against the *Times* and Farber.

James C. Goodale, vice chairman and general counsel of the New York Times Company, protested in the November 3, 1979 issue of *The Nation* that Farber and the *Times* had been victims of what the Columbia University Law School's Professor Benno Schmidt called an "outrageous miscarriage of justice." Under the New Jersey shield law, Goodale wrote, "Farber was entitled to the possession of his notes until a factual determination had been made that the statute had been waived or a legal determination that it was unconstitutional." And even if the statute did not apply, he continued, the First Amendment protected Farber "unless it could be shown Farber's notes were highly relevant and material" to Jascalevich's defense "and could be obtained from no other source." Goodale complained that "civil libertarians . . . hold the pervasive assumption than in a clash between the First and Sixth Amendments, the Sixth Amendment rights of the defendant must prevail, forgetting that Farber—who went to jail after all, without a fair hearing— has Sixth Amendment rights too."

Index

A

AGNEW, Spiro T. 16,19-23, 26, 28-9, 31, 35, 44, 49-51, 65-7, 86
ALIEN and Sedition Acts 7
AMERICAN Broadcasting Company (ABC) 35, 72, 82, 105, 115
AMERICAN Motors 92
AMERICAN Newspaper Guild 155
AMERICAN Telephone & Telegraph Company 114
ANDERSON, Glenn, M. 156
ANDERSON, Jack 76, 82
ARIZONA Republic 36
ARNOLD, William J. 171, 173
ATLANTA Constitution 28
ATLANTIC Monthly, The 127
ATTICA (correctional facilty) 30-1

B

BAGDIKIAN, Ben H. 79, 111
BALTIMORE Sun 27
BANCROFT, Harding 46
BARNER, Peter 109
BECKER Elizabeth 82
BELL v. *Wolfish* 131
BERNSTEIN, Carl 66
BEST, Hollis 170-71
BIRMINGHAM *News* 132
BIRNS, Harold 169
BLACK, Hugo L. 121-23, 135, 137
BLACKMUN, Harry A. 123, 126, 143-46, 148-49
BORN, Rosco C. 19
BOROSON, Warren 122
BORT, James H. 170
BOSTON Globe, The 36
BRADLEE, Benjamin 54, 57
BRAND, Stewart 79
BRANDEIS, Louis 16
BRANON, James 32-3
BRANZBURG, Paul M. 163
BRENNAN, Willian J. 120, 126, 128, 131, 143, 149
BRESLER, Charles S. 122
BRIDGE, Peter J. 169-70
BRINKLEY, David 22, 46
BROWN, Tyrone 105
BROWNE, Millard C. 108, 111
BUCHANAN, Patrick J. 44, 48, 59, 61 67, 82
BURCH, Dean 24-5, 46, 59, 87, 95-7
BURGER, Warren E. 11, 96, 123, 142, 146, 148
BURNETT, Carol 132-33
BURNETT, Lou Gehrig 32

C

CALDWELL, Earl 158-59, 161

175

CALLEY, William L. Jr. 138-39
CAMBODIA 82
CARMODY, Dierdre 155
CHANCELLOR, John 52-3
CHANDLER, Robert 91
CHAPLINSKY v. *New Hampshire* 6-7
CIRINO, Robert 79
CLARK, Tom C. 138
CLAWSON, Ken W. 68
COCKBURN, Alexander 84
COLE, Albert L. 65
COLSON, Charles 48, 61, 63
COLUMBIA Broadcasting System (CBS) 31, 35-6, 41-3, 52, 72, 82, 86, 91, 93, 103, 105, 115, 158; see also Paley, William
COLUMBIA Journalism Review 75
COMMITTEE to Defend Martin Luther King 120
CONCORD (New Hampshire) *Monitor* 122
COX, Archibald 68
CRONKITE, Walter 46, 52-3, 77
CURTIS, Thomas B. 65

D

DALEY, Richard J. 13
CAMRON, Leonard 123
DAVITT, John 86
DENNIS v. *United States* 8
DePASQUALE, Daniel A. 141-42
DES MOINES Register 129
DOLE, Robert 35
DOUGLAS, William O. 3, 121, 123, 166, 169, 170

E

EDITOR & Publisher 71
EHRLICHMAN, John 59
EISENHOWER, David 68
ELLIOTT, J. Robert 139
EMERSON, Thomas I. 5, 147
ERNST, Morris L. 107
ERVIN, Samuel J. 44, 5, 48, 167-68

F

FAIRNESS Doctrine 100-103
FARBER, Myron A. 171-72
FARR, William T. 170
FEDERAL Bureau of Investigation (FBI) 47-8
FEDERAL Communications Commission (FCC) 95-8, 100-05, 115-17
FEINGOLD, Benjamin F. 80
FERRIS, Charles D. 105
FLANIGAN, Peter 64

FRANK, Reuven 39
FRANKEL, Max 57
FRIENDLY, Fred W. 39-40, 47
FULBRIGHT, J. William 18-9, 43-4

G

GANNETT Company, The 113-14, 142, 145-46
GANNETT Co. v. *DePasquale* 141
GERTZ v. *Robert Welch, Inc.* 131
GILLMORE, Donald M. 12
GINZBURG, Ralph 122
GITLOW v. *New York* 8
GOLDBERG, Arthur J. 121
GOLDENSON, Leonard H. 24
GOLDWATER, Barry 121-22
GOODALE, James C. 173
GOODMAN, Julian 62-4
GOULD, Jack 31
GRAHAM, Katharine 28, 67
GRUNER, George F. 170
GRUNWALD, Henry 3
GURNEY, Edward J. 151

H

HALDEMAN, H.R. 58
HAMILL, Pete 28-9
HAMILTON, Andrew 4
HARLAN, John M. 123
HARTFORD (Connecticut) *Courant, The* 134
HAYAKOWA, S.I. 91
HEBERT, F. Edward 32-5, 40
HEDGE, Frank 92-3
HEISKELL, Andrew 3
HENKIN, Daniel Z. 34, 37, 42
HERBERT, Anthony B. 127
HERBERT v. *Lando* 127-31
HERBLOCK 28
HICKS, Dan Jr. 150
HIGBY, Lawrence 60-1
HILL, Alfred 121
HOFFER, Abram 80
HOLLINGS, Ernest F. 104
HOLMES, Oliver Wendell 8
HOOKER, John Jay Jr. 114
HORNER, Garnett 56
HOVING, Thomas P. 25
HUGHES, Charles Evans 147
HUNTLEY, Chet 60-1

J

JACKSON, Robert H. 9
JACOBSON, Michael 75
JEFFERSON, Thomas 6
JENSEN, Carl 78

JOHNSON, Malcolm "Mike" 89
JOHNSON, Nicholas 25, 46-7, 79, 98, 159
JONES, James 77

K

KALISH, Abraham H. 70-1, 77
KAMPELMAN, Max 10-11, 83, 87-8
KAUFMAN, Irving R. 127
KENNEDY, Edward M. 26
KENNEDY, J.P. 150
KENT State College 29
KHOMEINI, Ayatollah Ruhollah 90-1
KILLIAN, Johhny H. 157
KILPATRICK, James J. 11
KLEIN, Herbert G. 25,42, 48, 54, 57, 59, 60, 73
KRENTZMAN, Ben 151-52

L

LACEY, Frederick B. 172
LAIRD, Melvin, R. 35
LANDAU, Jack C. 128, 145, 150
LAQUEUR, Walter 90
LAW Enforcement Intelligence Unit 80
LEONARD, William A. 128, 132
LEWIS, Anthony 28
LEWIS, Ted 59
LIBEL 119-134
LIFE 158
LILIENTHAL, David E. 13
LINCOLN (Nebraska) *Star, The* 134
LIPPMAN, Walter 23
LISAGOR, Peter 57
LOOMIS, Henry 65
LOUISVILLE (Kentucky) *Courier-Journal* 134

M

MACKIN, Catherine 48
MacNEIL, John A. 34, 36
MacNEIL, Robert 64, 79
MADISON, James 6
MAGRUDER, Jeb S. 58-9, 61
MANCUSO, Thomas 79
MARCHETTI, Victor 79
MARKEL, Lester 69
MARSHALL, Thurgood 117, 123, 126, 128, 130, 143, 148
MASTERSON, William A. 133
McGRORY, Mary 79
McHUGH, Raymond 56
McLAUGHLIN, Walter 151
MEDIA Access Project 105
MIAMI Herald Publishing Co. v. *U.S.* 151
MINNEAPOLIS Tribune 130

MINNESOTA Newspaper Association 49
MITCHELL, John N. 158-59
MITFORD, Jessica 79
MOLLENHOFF, Clark R. 25, 56
MONROE, Bill 48, 100
MOORE, Thomas W. 65
MUDD, Roger 31, 34, 44
MURROW, Edward R. 39

N

NASHVILLE Banner 113
NATIONAL Academy of Television Arts & Sciences 43
NATIONAL Association of Broadcasters 42
NATIONAL Broadcasting Company (NBC) 35, 72, 101-04, 114-15
NBC v. *United States* 95
NATIONAL Citizens Committee for Broadcasting 117
NATIONAL Commission on the Causes & Prevention of Violence 71
NATIONAL Educational Television (NET) 64
NATIONAL *Enquirer* 132-34
NATIONAL Press Club 34, 73
NATIONAL Public Affairs Center 64
NEAR v. *Minnesota* 147
NEBRASKA Press Association v. *Stuart* 147
NELSON, Harold L. 12
NELSON, Jack 79
NEUHARTH, Allen H. 129, 145
NEW Republic 28
NEWSDAY 130
NEWSPAPER Preservation Act 108
NEWS Review 122
NEWSWEEK 48, 158
NEW York Daily News 140
NEW York *Daily Times* 81
NEW York Post, 28, 37, 81, 140
NEW York Times, The 27-8, 46, 64, 68, 72, 77, 120, 140, 158, 173
NEW York Times v. *Sullivan* 119-20, 127, 131
NIXON, Richard M. 16, 28, 44, 66, 155
NIXON Administration 15-67
passim; see also specific individuals
NOFZIGER, Franklin C. 61
NORTH American Newspaper Alliance 122
NOVAK, Robert 56
NUTRITIONAL Scoreboard: Your Guide to Better Eating 75
NUTRITION Today 75
NYE, Russel B. 73

O

OAKES, James L. 127

OAKES, John B. 10, 108
O'BRIEN, Lawrence F. 62
OCALA (Florida) *Star-Banner* 123
OFFICE of Communications of United Church of Christ v. *FCC* 96
OKLAHOMA Publishing Co. v. *District Court* 151
OLDER, Charles C. 170
OPOTOWSKY, Stan 91
OREGONIAN 36
OTTEN, Alan 35, 56

P

PALEY, William S. 52, 62, 115
PAN American Airways 94
PAPPAS, Paul 163
PATTERSON v. *Colorado* 8
PATTERSON, William K. 170
PEARSON, Drew 122
PEARSON, James B. 47
PECKINPAH, Denver C. 171
PEMBER, Don R. 12
PENTAGON Propaganda Machine 43
PERCY, Charles 60
PERLIK, Charles A. Jr. 156, 169
PERSICO, Carmine 139-41
PINSKY, Mark 84
PLANER, Ed 91
POLLACK, Ronald 75-6
POL Pot 82
POORMAN, Paul 93
POWELL, Lewis F. 128, 142-43, 146, 148, 150
PRESSLER, Larry 109, 110
PROVIDENCE (R.I.) Journal, The 36
PROXMIRE, William 67, 102
PUBLIC Broadcasting Service 64

R

RADIO Corporation of America (RCA) 114
RATHER, Dan 56
RAUSCH, James S. 88
RAYMONT, Henry 157
REHNQUIST, William H. 126, 142-43, 147-48
REASONER, Harry 52
RED Lion Broadcasting Co. v. *FCC* 96, 98, 117
REES, John 83-4
REID, Tom 131
REPUBLICAN National Committee 35
RESTON, James 28
RICHARDSON, Elliot 160
RICHMOND Newspapers v. *Virginia* 146
ROGERS, Jimmie N. 43
ROSATO, Joe 171

ROSENBLATT, Maurice 109
ROSENTHAL, A.M. 156
ROSSANT, M.J. 72
ROWAN, Carl T. 28
ROWE, James 33
ROY, Alphonse 123
RUMANIA 94

S

ST. LOUIS Post-Dispatch 36
SALANT, Richard 35, 37-8, 43, 72, 86
SALT Lake Tribune, The 130
SAMUELSON, Robert W. 75-6
SAN Diego Union, The 37
SANFORD, Bruce W. 131
SARNOFF, David 115
SATURDAY Review 42
SAXE, Susan 150
SYRE, Dean 54
SCHLESINGER, Arthur Jr. 49
SCHMIDT, Richard 150
SCHORR, Daniel 47-8
SCHULINGKAMP, Oliver P. 150
SCHWAB, Joseph J. 79
SEIB, Charles E. 89
"SELLING of the Pentagon, The" 31-44
SEMPLE, Robert B. Jr. 44
SENTINEL Star 134
SEVAREID, Eric 76-8
SHAW, Charles 11
SHELLEDY, James E. (Jay) 171
SHENEFIELD, John H. 110
SHEPPARD, Samuel H. 136-38
SHUMWAY, DeVan 58
SIDEY, Hugh 28, 59
SIEGENTHALER, John 112
SIMANTS, Erwin Charles 148
SIMONTON, James 156
SMALL, Bill 48
SMITH, Howard K. 25, 52, 59
SOLZHENITSYN, Alexander 76
STAGGERS, Harley O. 41-2, 84-5
STANTON, Frank 24, 41-2, 46, 62, 86
STAR-LEDGER 129
STERN, Lawrence 82
STEVENS, John Paul 142, 146, 149
STEWART, Potter 16-7, 122-23, 128, 142, 149, 165
STONE, Marvin L. 109, 115
STRUGGLE for Freedom in the South 120
STUART, Connie 60
STUART, Hugh 148
SULLIVAN, L.B. 120
SULZBERGER, Arthur Ochs 27, 72
SUPREME Court 117, 122-23, 126-27, 141, 146, 148, 151-52; see also specific members

T

TENNESSEAN 113

THORNBURGH, Richard L.   135
THREE Mile Island   81
TIME   123, 158
TIMES Co. v. *Suillivan*   97
TIMES-Picayune   132
TRAUTWEIN, Theodore W.   171-72
TRAYNOR, Roger J.   72
TRIBUNE Publishing Co. v. *Caldero*   171
TROHAN, Walter   59
TRUMAN, Harry S.   13
TSCHANTZ, Bruce A.   80
TUNNEY, John V.   136, 148
TWENTIETH Century Fund   72

U

UNITED Press International (UPI)   88
UNITED States, Petitioner, v. *Earl Caldwell*   162-63

V

VANOCUR, Sander   64
VILLAGE Voice   169

W

WALLACE, Mike   92-4, 127, 159
WALL Street Journal   83
WARREN, Gerald L.   67
WASHINGTON Post,   27-8, 37, 46, 77, 82, 89
WEAF   114
WEAVER, Paul H.   87

WEST Virginia State Board of Education v. *Barnette*   9
WEIDENFELD, Shelia   79
WEINMAN, Carl A.   137
WESTINGHOUSE Corporation   114
WHALEN, Charles W.   47
WHITE, Byron R.   98, 122-23, 127-28, 143, 148, 163
WHITEHEAD, Clay   48, 65
WHITTEN, Les   76
WICKER, Tom   28, 129
WIGGINS, James Russell   12
WILEY, Richard W.   104
WITZE, Claude   34
WOLSTON v. *Reader's Digest Association, Inc.*   126
WOODS, Donald   82
WOODS, William C.   32
WOODWARD, Bob   66
WRATHER, Jack   65

Y

YATHAY, Pin   82

Z

ZEITLIN, Maurice   81
ZEMEL v. *Rusk*   164
ZENGER, John Peter   4
ZIEGLER, Ronald L.   66-7
ZION, Sidney   11
ZIRPOLI, Alfonzo J.   161
ZWERDLING, Daniel   79

FUNDERBURG LIBRARY
MANCHESTER COLLEGE